Day Wal
Snowdonia

20 circular routes in North Wales

VERTEBRATE **PUBLISHING**

Design and production by Vertebrate Publishing, Sheffield
www.**v-publishing**.co.uk

Day Walks in Snowdonia

20 circular routes in North Wales

Written by
Tom Hutton

Day Walks in Snowdonia

20 circular routes in North Wales

Published by Vertebrate Publishing

ISBN 978-1-906148-41-6

Cover photo: Glyder Fawr from Llyn Idwal.
Back cover photo: Llyn Crafnant from near Crimpiau.

All Photography by **Tom Hutton.**

Design and production by Nathan Ryder.
www.v-graphics.co.uk

Printed in China.

Contents

CWM IDWAL

Introduction

It's sometimes said that Snowdonia is Wales in miniature but in my opinion this is both lazy and inaccurate and fails to do justice to the grandeur of the largest and most spectacular of the principality's national parks.

It would be closer to the truth to describe Snowdonia as Wales in caricature – the features are the same but somehow the small seems smaller and the large, larger. The flora appears more delicate and fragile, the rivers seem faster and more tumultuous, the ridges are sharper and narrower and, of course, the mountains are higher. To me, walking among these mountains is as much a sensory experience as a physical one.

And I hope the walks in the book will inspire the reader as much as they do me.

For ease of use, I have divided the guide into three sections: Northern, Central and Southern Snowdonia, although it has to be said that the boundaries are fairly arbitrary.

The northern section, which makes up the lion's share of the book, covers the highest mountains, which are spread across three dramatic mountain ranges. The Carneddau is the largest of Snowdonia's massifs and contains the most ground above the 1,000m contour line; the Glyderau is definitely the most rocky – a trait that makes it exceptionally popular with scramblers and climbers as well as walkers; and the Snowdon Massif is of course home to the highest peak.

The central section takes in the Nantlle Hills and the Moelwynion, both of which nestle up against the northern peaks but offer walking of a very different character; as well as the wild and rugged north-south ridge of the Rhinogydd, perhaps the toughest walking in the national park; and the outlying Arenig Hills, which stretch away to the eastern boundary.

Southern Snowdonia is dominated by Cadair Idris, perhaps the only mountain in Wales that is truly as spectacular from the south as it is from the north, but the nearby Arans reach higher, offering a wonderful wilderness experience, and the grassy outlier of Rhobell Fawr is definitely worth exploring too; if only for the solitude.

The walks all take in summits. Somehow days in the mountains don't seem quite complete without a cairn or trig point to touch. But they don't necessarily take the easiest routes to the top; instead exploring the best of the surrounding scenery, often visiting hidden lakes or secret cwms that would otherwise be missed.

And finally a word on scrambling: the northern mountains are justly famed for their excellent scrambling as well as their walking, so no book covering this region would be complete without a mention of the best of these. For that reason I've included a round of the wonderful Snowdon Horseshoe and an ascent of Tryfan's dramatic north ridge in a bonus section. Both are easily achievable by agile walkers with a head for heights, especially when the weather's good; but neither should be taken lightly. If you've not scrambled before, it's probably best to get a few of the other walks under your belt first before you start on these.

Tom Hutton

Acknowledgements

Thanks to Steph and Du for their company in the hills and their support when I'm stuck in the office. And to all the wonderful friends I've shared a summit with over the years.

About the walks

What is a day walk? For the purposes of this book, it's a walk that will take up the majority of a day for an averagely fit walker. The shortest walks could definitely be squeezed into a morning, afternoon or evening if you're fast; and the longest could see you finishing in the dark in winter.

Most of the walks follow clear paths for most of their length but there are many trackless sections in these mountains and also one or two steep sections, where a trip could be catastrophic. All take in at least one summit, and usually more.

All the walks are within the capabilities of a reasonably fit walker but involve a lot of up and down and assume at least a little previous experience. The scrambles in the *Bonus Section* definitely require a head for heights. If you are in any doubt, study the walk description before deciding whether a walk is for you.

Walk times

The times given are reasonably generous while giving a guideline for planning purposes. If you're unsure how fast or slow you walk, start off with one of the shorter routes and progress to the longer ones once you're sure.

Winter

In full winter conditions, i.e. with snow and ice on the ground, these walks could all become serious mountaineering adventures and should only be attempted by walkers with the relevant experience and correct equipment, for example ice axe and crampons.

Navigation

As a rule, the description and map included should be enough to get around safely and accurately, but it's always worth carrying a back-up copy of the relevant OS or Harvey Map, in case you inadvertently travel off the page, or need to change your route for any reason.

Snowdonia National Park is covered by the following maps:
Ordnance Survey Explorer OL17 (1:25,000), Snowdon
Ordnance Survey Explorer OL18 (1:25,000), Harlech, Porthmadog & Bala
Ordnance Survey Explorer OL23 (1:25,000), Cadair Idris & Llyn Tegid

Harvey/BMC British Mountain Map Snowdonia (1:40,000)
Harvey/BMC British Mountain Map Snowdonia South (1:40,000)

A compass and the basic ability to use it should be seen as prerequisite to walking in the high mountains even if you are carrying a GPS.

GPS

A GPS can be a useful navigational aid and is well worth carrying. But always carry spare batteries – they do tend to run out at the worst times – and always carry a map and compass as back up.

Mobile Phones

Mobile phone reception is at best iffy in the mountains so it's definitely best not to rely on it. If you do need to make contact with emergency services, try heading up towards a summit, where you often have more chance of a signal.

Footpaths and rights of way

The walks in this book all follow rights of way, permissive paths or cross open access land.

Comfort

A decent pair of boots will protect your feet from the kind of terrain experienced in high mountains and will also provide ankle support, waterproofing and grip on steep slopes. And a waterproof jacket could be useful on any day at any time of year. A pack containing a waterproof, spare layer and some food and drink, will make any day more comfortable. Anybody with joint problems, for example ankles or knees, will probably benefit from a pair of trekking poles.

Safety

Mountain weather changes quickly and unexpectedly, if you are in any doubt, it's probably best not to start, and if you do get caught out, it's always better to back off your route rather than carry on regardless. The mountains will always be there. In winter, consider carrying a torch in case the light fades before you get off the hill – it's difficult reading a map in the dark.

Mountain Rescue

In case of an emergency dial **999** and ask for **Police** and then **Mountain Rescue**. Where possible give a 6-figure grid reference of your location or that of the casualty. If you don't have reception where you are, try and attract the help of others around you. The usual distress signal is six short blasts on a whistle every minute. If you don't have a whistle, then shouting may work.

Mountain Rescue by SMS Text

Another option in the UK is contacting the emergency services by SMS text – useful if you have a low battery or intermittent signal, but you do need to register your phone first. To register, simply text **'register'** to 999 and then follow the instructions in the reply. Do it now – it could save yours or someone else's life. **www.emergencysms.org.uk**

The Countryside Code

Be safe – plan ahead

Even when going out locally, it's best to get the latest information about where and when you can go; for example, your rights to go onto some areas of open land may be restricted while work is carried out, for safety reasons or during breeding and shooting seasons. Follow advice and local signs, and be prepared for the unexpected.

- Refer to up-to-date maps or guidebooks.
- You're responsible for your own safety and for others in your care, so be prepared for changes in weather and other events.
- There are many organisations offering specific advice on equipment and safety, or contact visitor information centres and libraries for a list of outdoor recreation groups.
- Check weather forecasts before you leave, and don't be afraid to turn back.
- Part of the appeal of the countryside is that you can get away from it all. You may not see anyone for hours and there are many places without clear mobile phone signals, so let someone else know where you're going and when you expect to return.

Leave gates and property as you find them

Please respect the working life of the countryside, as our actions can affect people's livelihoods, our heritage, and the safety and welfare of animals and ourselves.

- A farmer will normally leave a gate closed to keep livestock in, but may sometimes leave it open so they can reach food and water. Leave gates as you find them or follow instructions on signs; if walking in a group, make sure the last person knows how to leave the gates.
- In fields where crops are growing, follow the paths wherever possible.
- Use gates and stiles wherever possible – climbing over walls, hedges and fences can damage them and increase the risk of farm animals escaping.
- Our heritage belongs to all of us – be careful not to disturb ruins and historic sites.
- Leave machinery and livestock alone – don't interfere with animals even if you think they're in distress. Try to alert the farmer instead.

Protect plants and animals, and take your litter home

We have a responsibility to protect our countryside now and for future generations, so make sure you don't harm animals, birds, plants or trees.

- » Litter and leftover food doesn't just spoil the beauty of the countryside, it can be dangerous to wildlife and farm animals and can spread disease – so take your litter home with you. Dropping litter and dumping rubbish are criminal offences.
- » Discover the beauty of the natural environment and take special care not to damage, destroy or remove features such as rocks, plants and trees. They provide homes and food for wildlife, and add to everybody's enjoyment of the countryside.
- » Wild animals and farm animals can behave unpredictably if you get too close, especially if they're with their young – so give them plenty of space.
- » Fires can be as devastating to wildlife and habitats as they are to people and property – so be careful not to drop a match or smouldering cigarette at any time of the year. Sometimes, controlled fires are used to manage vegetation, particularly on heaths and moors between October and early April, so please check that a fire is not supervised before calling 999.

Keep dogs under close control

The countryside is a great place to exercise dogs, but it is the owner's duty to make sure their dog is not a danger or nuisance to farm animals, wildlife or other people.

- » By law, you must control your dog so that it does not disturb or scare farm animals or wildlife. You must keep your dog on a short lead on most areas of open country and common land between 1 March and 31 July, and at all times near farm animals.
- » You do not have to put your dog on a lead on public paths as long as it is under close control. But as a general rule, keep your dog on a lead if you cannot rely on its obedience. By law, farmers are entitled to destroy a dog that injures or worries their animals.
- » If a farm animal chases you and your dog, it is safer to let your dog off the lead – don't risk getting hurt by trying to protect it.
- » Take particular care that your dog doesn't scare sheep and lambs or wander where it might disturb birds that nest on the ground and other wildlife – eggs and young will soon die without protection from their parents.
- » Everyone knows how unpleasant dog mess is and it can cause infections – so always clean up after your dog and get rid of the mess responsibly. Also make sure your dog is wormed regularly.

Consider other people

Showing consideration and respect for other people makes the countryside a pleasant environment for everyone – at home, at work and at leisure.

» Busy traffic on small country roads can be unpleasant and dangerous to local people, visitors and wildlife – so slow down and, where possible, leave your vehicle at home, consider sharing lifts and use alternatives such as public transport or cycling. For public transport information, phone Traveline on 0871 200 2233.
» Respect the needs of local people – for example, don't block gateways, driveways or other entry points with your vehicle.
» By law, cyclists must give way to walkers and horse riders on bridleways.
» Keep out of the way when farm animals are being gathered or moved and follow directions from the farmer.
» Support the rural economy – for example, buy your supplies from local shops.

How to use this book

This book should provide you with all of the information that you need for an enjoyable, trouble free and successful walk. The following tips should also be of help:

1. We strongly recommend that you invest in the maps listed above on page ix. These are essential even if you are familiar with the area – you may need to cut short the walk or take an alternative route.

2. Choose your route. Consider the time you have available and the abilities/level of experience of all of members your party – then read the safety section of this guide.

3. We recommend that you study the route description carefully before setting off. Cross-reference this with your OS map so that you've got a good sense of general orientation in case you need an escape route. Make sure that you are familiar with the symbols used on the maps.

4. Get out there and get walking!

Maps, Descriptions, Distances

While every effort has been made to maintain accuracy within the maps and descriptions in this guide, we have had to process a vast amount of information and we are unable to guarantee that every single detail is correct.

Please exercise caution if a direction appears at odds with the route on the map. If in doubt, a comparison between the route, the description and a quick cross-reference with your OS map (along with a bit of common sense) should help ensure that you're on the right track. Note that distances have been measured off the map, and map distances rarely coincide 100% with distances on the ground. Please treat stated distances as a guideline only.

Ordnance Survey maps are the most commonly used, are easy to read and many people are happy using them. If you're not familiar with OS maps and are unsure of what the symbols mean, you can download a free OS 1:25,000 map legend from **www.v-outdoor.co.uk**

Here are a few of the symbols and abbreviations we use on the maps and in our directions:

ROUTE STARTING POINT

ROUTE MARKER

OPTIONAL ROUTE

52 ADDITIONAL GRID LINE NUMBERS TO AID NAVIGATION

PB = public bridleway; **PF** = public footpath; **GR** = grid reference.

Km/mile conversion chart

Metric to Imperial

1 kilometre [km]	1000 m	0.6214 mile
1 metre [m]	100 cm	1.0936 yd
1 centimetre [cm]	10 mm	0.3937 in
1 millimetre [mm]		0.03937 in

Imperial to Metric

1 mile	1760 yd	1.6093 km
1 yard [yd]	3 ft	0.9144 m
1 foot [ft]	12 in	0.3048 m
1 inch [in]		2.54 cm

The Welsh Language (Cymraeg)

In a perfect world, we'd have produced this book in two languages but who wants to climb a mountain with a book that's twice as heavy and thick as it needs to be in their pocket? We have in the text, however, tried to explain meanings and pronunciations of key Welsh words to help non-speakers get a little insight into the local lingo, which is one of the oldest languages in Europe. The glossary opposite will also assist with the understanding of many of the place names mentioned. We hope the non Welsh speakers find this helpful and interesting, and that it meets with the approval of those that do speak the language.

Yr Iaith Gymraeg

Mewn byd perffaith, bydden ni wedi cyfieithu'r llyfr hwn i'r ddwy iaith, ond pwy sydd eisiau dringo mynydd gyda llyfr yn ei poced sydd ddwy waith mor drwm a sydd angen? Wedi dweud hynny, rydyn ni wedi ceisio esbonio ystyron rhai o brif eiriau'r Gymraeg, a sut i'w ynganu, er mwyn rhoi agoriad llygad i'r iaith lleol, yr iaith Ewropeaidd hynaf sy'n dal i gael ei ddefnyddio. Bydd y rhestr isod yn eich helpu i ddeall ystyr rhai o enwau'r lleoedd rydyn ni'n eu crybwyll. Rydyn ni'n gobeithio bydd y rhestr hon yn ddefnyddiol ac yn ddiddorol, ac yn dderbyniol i'r rhai hynny sydd yn siarad yr iaith Gymraeg.

Aber — Confluence or mouth of a river
Afon — River
Bach (also **Fach**) — Small
Betws — House of prayer
Blaen — Head of a valley
Bont (also **Pont**) — Bridge
Bryn — Hill
Bwlch — Pass or gap
Capel — Chapel
Carn — Pile of stones
Carreg — Stone
Castell — Castle
Cefn — Ridge
Coch — Red
Coed — Wood
Craig — Crag
Cwm — Valley or cirque
Dan (also **Tan**) — Below
Dwr — Water
Eglwys — Church
Esgair — Ridge
Fawr (also **Mawr**) — Big
Foel (also **Moel**) — Bare hill
Ffridd — Pasture
Ffordd — Road
Ffynnon — Well or spring
Glan — Bank or shore
Glyn — Valley
Hafod — Summer dwelling or pasture
Hen — Old
Isaf — Lower
Llan — A church, usually followed by the name of the saint to whom it's dedicated
Llwyn — A bush or grove
Llyn — Lake
Maes — Field
Mynydd (also **Fynydd**) — Mountain
Nant — Stream
Pant — Hollow
Pen — Top or end
Pentre — Village
Pwll — Pool
Rhiw — Slope
Rhos — Moorland
Rhyd — Ford
Tal — End or front
Tre (also **Tref**) — Homestead or town
Ty — House
Uchaf — Higher
Waun — Moorland or meadow
Ynys — Island
Ystrad — Wide valley

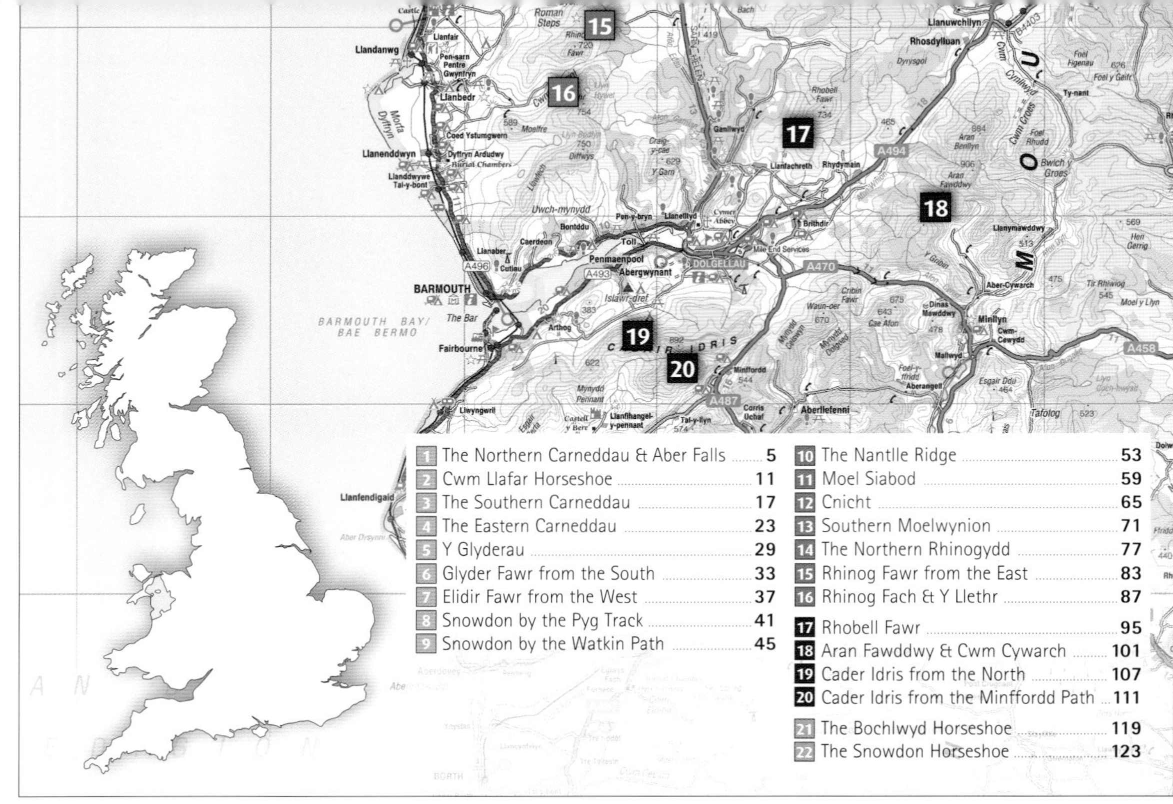
Llandanwg
Llanfair
Pen-sarn
Pentre
Gwynfryn
Llanbedr
Morfa Dyffryn
Coed Ystumgwern
Llanenddwyn
Dyffryn Ardudwy
Llanddwywe
Tal-y-bont
Uwch-mynydd
Bontddu
Caerdeon
Llanaber
BARMOUTH
BARMOUTH BAY/
BAE BERMO
The Bar
Fairbourne
Arthog
Islawr-dref
Penmaenpool
Abergwynant
Pen-y-bryn
Llanelltyd
Cymer Abbey
Toll
DOLGELLAU
Mile End Services
Brithdir
Ganllwyd
Llanfachreth
Rhydymain
Rhobell Fawr
Llanuwchllyn
Rhosdylluan
Aran Benllyn
Aran Fawddwy
Llanymawddwy
Aber-Cywarch
Dinas Mawddwy
Minllyn
Cwm-Cewydd
Mallwyd
Aberangell
Aberllefenni
Corris Uchaf
Minffordd
Tal-y-llyn
Llanfihangel-y-pennant
Llwyngwril
Llanfendigaid
Roman Steps
A496
A493
A470
A494
A487
A458
B4403
15
16
17
18
19
20

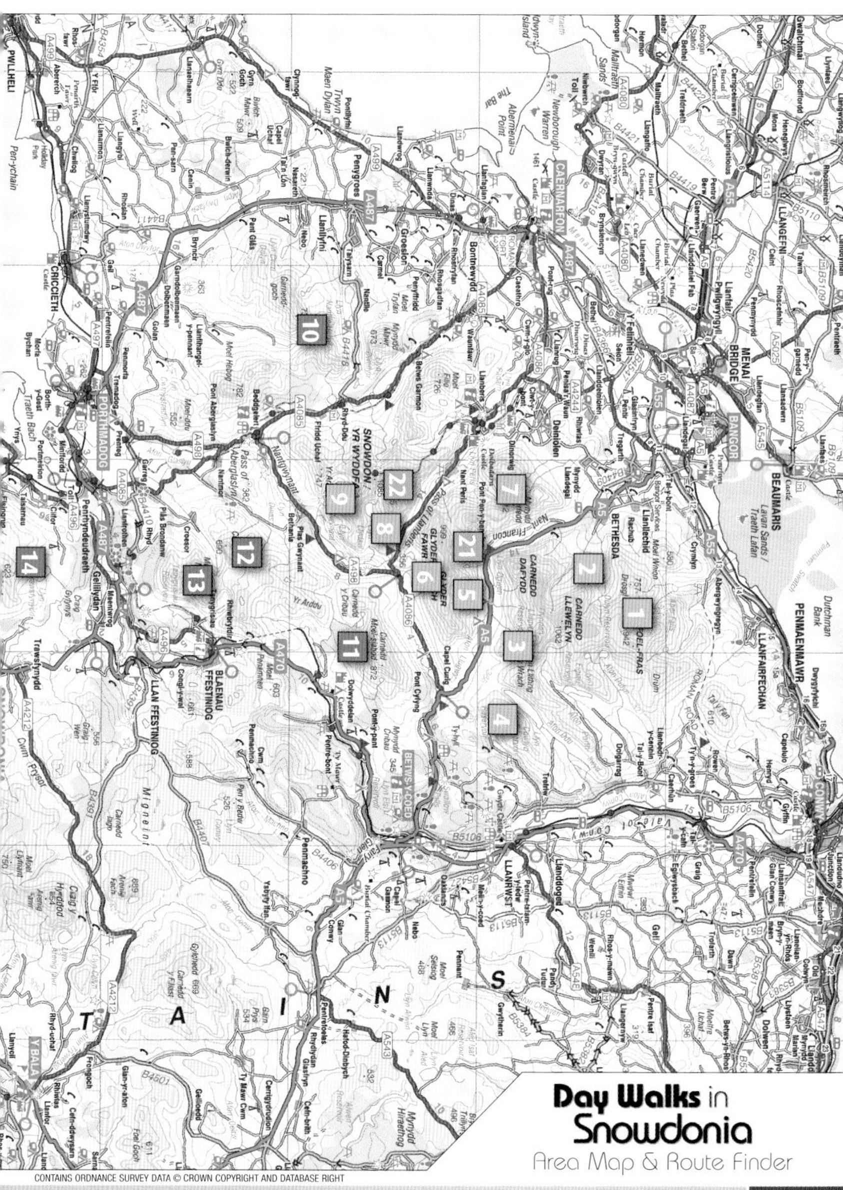
Day Walks in
Snowdonia
Area Map & Route Finder

SECTION 1

Northern Snowdonia

These walks are all in the northernmost massifs of the national park and cross the highest most demanding ground. Each is very different: the Carneddau is very high but the summits and ridges are rounded and generally grassy; the Glyderau, on the other hand, is a jumble of boulders on the top, flanked by some of Wales's most impressive rock architecture; the Snowdon Massif has a little of everything including, of course, the highest mountain in England and Wales.

THE IMPOSING EAST FACE OF TRYFAN

CWM LLAFAR

THE NORTHERN CARNEDDAU & ABER FALLS

DISTANCE: 17KM/10.5MILES » **TOTAL ASCENT:** 970M/3,182FT » **START GR:** SH 663719 » **TIME:** 6–7 HOURS **MAP:** OS EXPLORER OL17 SNOWDON » **REFRESHMENTS:** CAFÉ HENFELIN, ABERGWYNGREGYN » **TRANSPORT:** BUSES BETWEEN ABERGWYNGREGYN AND BANGOR OR LLANFAIRFECHAN AND RAIL LINKS WITH BOTH OF THESE TOWNS. **NAVIGATION:** STRAIGHTFORWARD BUT SOME TRACKLESS GOING ON INITIAL ASCENT AND ALSO ON THE DESCENT FROM GARNEDD UCHAF.

CASCADES ON THE AFON GOCH

01 The Northern Carneddau & Aber Falls

17km/10.5miles

A remote expedition over Snowdonia's northernmost summits

Bont Newydd » Afon Goch » Foel Fras (942m) » Carnedd Gwenllian (926m) » Bera Bach » Aber Falls » Bont Newydd

Start

Pay and display at the Aber Falls Car Park, Bont Newydd, 1km south of the A55 at Abergwyngregyn. GR: SH 663719.

The Walk

The northern peaks of the Carneddau are quite different to the main summits just a little further south. Whereas Carnedd Llewelyn and Carnedd Dafydd, the two highest mountains in the range, are joined by a narrow, airy ridge that dips deeply into a broad dividing col; the tops of Foel Fras and Carnedd Gwenllian are kept apart by a broad grassy shoulder that falls less than 50m from either. This shouldn't put anyone off though – this is still very high ground and it's an exhilarating place to walk.

This is an outing of contrasts, starting close to one of the area's biggest tourist draws – Aber Falls – and then breaking away into something resembling a true wilderness beyond. The opening section is trampled by as many trainers as it is walking boots, but the dog-walkers and the 2.5-children families are soon left behind and the initial clamber alongside the banks of the beautiful tumbling Afon Goch will almost certainly be a lonely affair.

It gets rougher the higher you get, and most will be relieved when they finally stumble upon a semblance of a path as they reach the spine of the ridge proper. It's then an easy task to link the two summits before starting on the descent. This follows good paths most of the way, though there's plenty of opportunity to freelance should you wish. The grand finale is a visit to Aber Falls – a true spectacle in spate and a great place to finish off your sarnies before the easy walk back down to the bridge.

Incidentally, Carnedd Gwenllian is a recently adopted name for the mountain previously known as Garnedd Uchaf. Gwenllian was the daughter of the last Prince of an independent Wales, Llewelyn ap Gruffydd and his wife Eleanor, after whom Carnedd Llewelyn and Yr Elen are named. Carnedd Dafydd is named after Llewlyn's brother. It's certainly a more fitting title for Snowdonia's 14th highest peak than Garnedd Uchaf, which translates to Highest Cairn.

BERA MAWR AND THE AFON GOCH

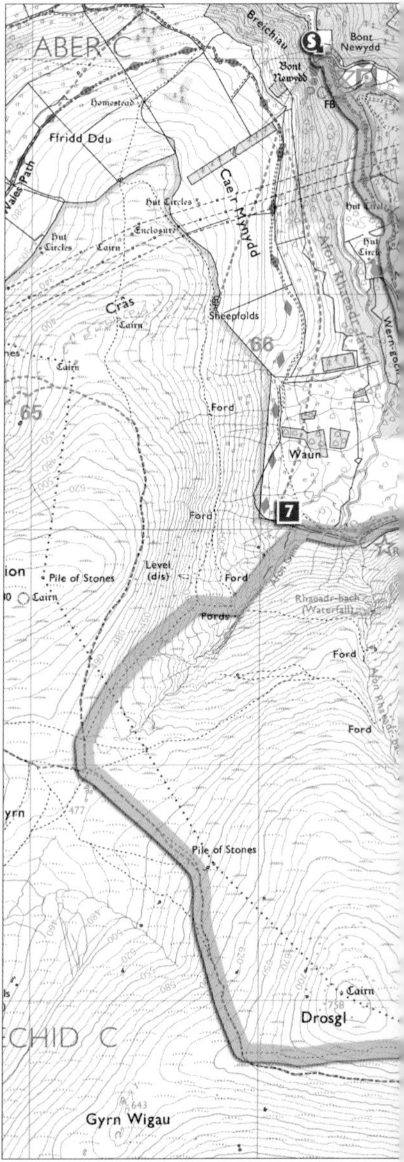

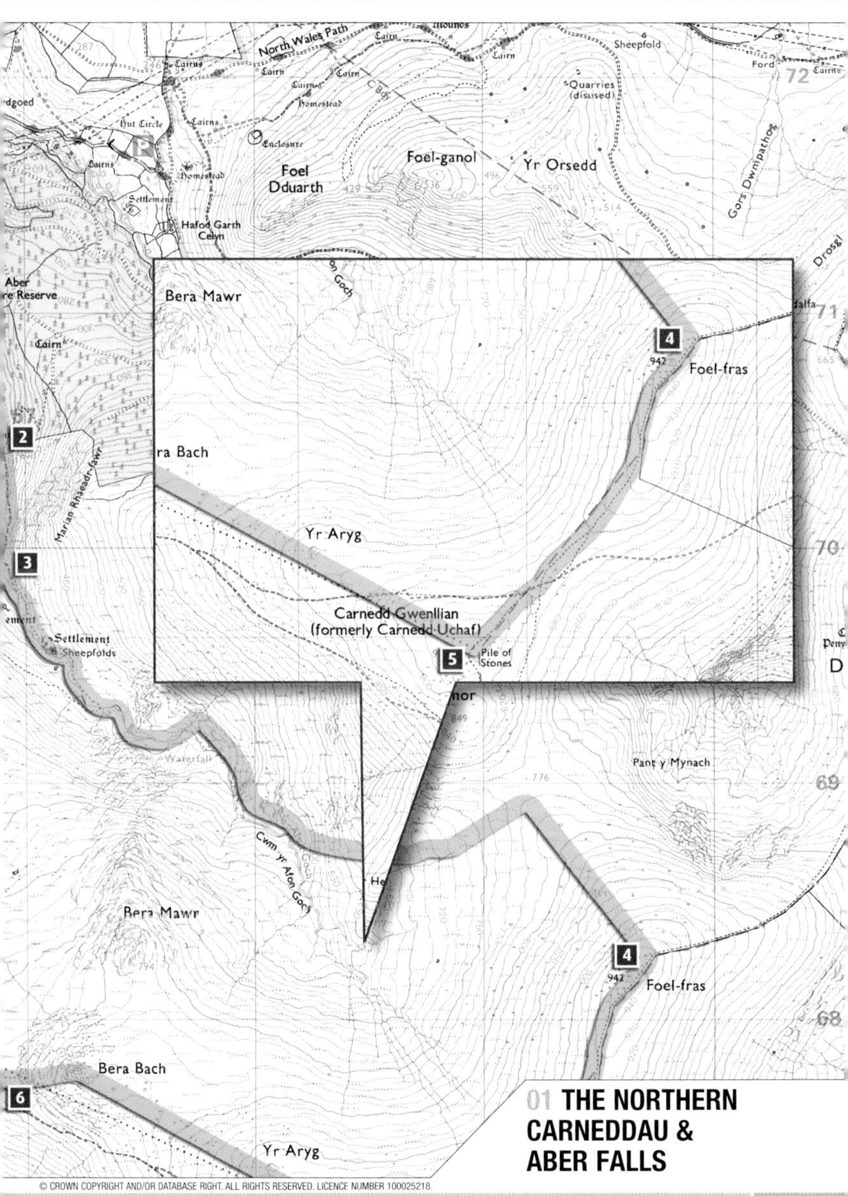

01 THE NORTHERN CARNEDDAU & ABER FALLS

Directions – The Northern Carneddau & Aber Falls

S Go through the gate and follow the main track upstream and over the bridge, where it then merges with a track. **Bear right** onto this to continue uphill to a fork, where you take the **left turn**, signed to Aber Falls through the wood. Follow this until it emerges from the wood and then keep **straight ahead** over a ladder stile, where the main path to the falls now drops to the right.

2 Don't take this but instead **keep ahead** to follow a clear path that traverses the steep slope before continuing along an exposed section, high above the stream. Now follow this, always with the stream on your right, until it eventually levels slightly and enters the remote Cwm yr Afon Goch.

3 Ahead now are the rocky summits of Llwytmor to the left and Bera Mawr to the right. Continue ever upwards, hugging the stream bank as tight as possible until, after passing above a lovely gorge, you **bear half left** to freelance your way up the grassy hillside to a saddle between Llwytmor and Foel-Fras. Once in the saddle, **bear right** to the trig point atop Foel-fras (942m).

4 Continue alongside the wall **(SW)** and you'll drop into a shallow dip before climbing easily again to the summit of Carnedd Gwenllian (926m). The jumbled rocks of the summit make a good place to take a breather before moving on.

5 Now leave the main path, which heads towards Foel Grach and head **north-west**, where you'll pick up a faint path that leads over the rocky tor of Yr Aryg to the next tor – Bera Bach. Continue west to pick up a good track that heads directly into the saddle beyond the rugged hilltop of Drosgl.

6 Continue into this saddle and pass beneath the summit before continuing **north-west** towards another saddle; this one at the foot of Moel Wnion. Continue across the floor of the saddle until you pass the head of the Afon Gam and then **bear right** to follow intermittent paths downstream, keeping the waterway to your right the whole time.

7 At the bottom of the descent, you need to cross the stream and continue to a ladder stile that gives access to a good path that will now carry you east to Aber Falls. From here, cross the bridge and follow the track back down to the car park.

YR ELEN FROM FFYNNON CASEG

02 Cwm Llafar Horseshoe

17km/10.5miles

The Carneddau's highest peaks from a secluded valley to the west

Gerlan » Afon Llafar » Mynydd Du » Carnedd Dafydd (1,044m) » Carnedd Llewelyn (1,064m) » Yr Elen (962m) » Afon Caseg » Gerlan

Start

Limited parking in Gerlan Village, close to the village shop, or alternatively, Bethesda. Bethesda is on the A5, a few kilometres south of Bangor. GR: SH 632664.

The Walk

This is one of those walks that once you're up you stay up, with only minimal height gain and loss between the three big peaks that form the crux of it. The main climb comes from the start – first up onto the banks of the Afon Llafar, where the gradient relents temporarily to allow you to bathe in the ambience of a majestic valley; and then on the long pull over Mynydd Du to the range's second in command, Carnedd Dafydd. From here it's an airy walkway above the notorious Ysgolion Duon (the Black Ladders) before a final steep climb deposits you on the 1,064m summit of Carnedd Llewelyn.

This is a great place from where to admire the rugged loftiness of the Carneddau range, which is so different in character to the nearby Glyderau, on the other side of the Ogwen Valley. To the north, the ridge continues over Foel Grach towards Carnedd Gwenllian and the peaks climbed by Walk 01, and to the east, things funnel down into a narrow saddle, Bwlch Eryl Farchog, which crowns one of Snowdonia's most impressive crags – Craig yr Ysfa (see Walk 03). But this outing turns to the west now, where Yr Elen – surely the shapeliest of the Carneddau peaks – marks the end of the skyline section.

The descent of Yr Elen's north east ridge leads to one of Snowdonia's truly special places: the hidden tarn of Ffynnon Caseg, and from here, it's a simple job of following the stream that issues from it back down towards Gerlan. Things are never quite as easy as they seem though and the upper sections of the route are pathless and occasionally awkward to navigate.

CWM LLAFAR HORSESHOE

DISTANCE: 17KM/10.5MILES » **TOTAL ASCENT:** 1,160M/3,805FT » **START GR:** SH 632664 » **TIME:** 6–7 HOURS **MAP:** OS EXPLORER OL17 SNOWDON » **REFRESHMENTS:** PLENTY OF CHOICE IN BETHESDA » **TRANSPORT:** BUSES TO BETHESDA AND GERLAN » **NAVIGATION:** STRAIGHTFORWARD FOR MOST OF THE WALK BUT THINGS CAN GET A BIT AWKWARD TOWARDS THE END WHERE ONLY FAINT PATHS LEAD DOWN STEEP, GRASSY HILLSIDES ALONGSIDE THE INFANT AFON CASEG. A GOOD PATH EVENTUALLY ESTABLISHES ITSELF ON THE NORTH SIDE OF THE STREAM.

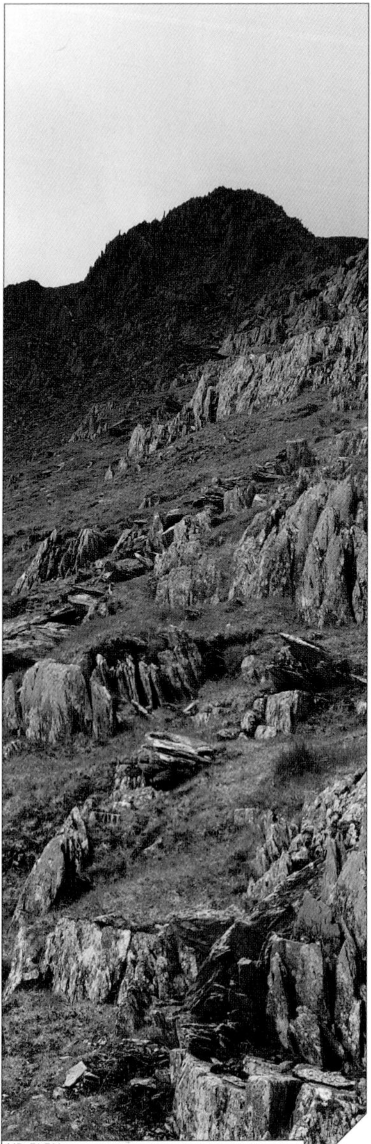

YR ELEN

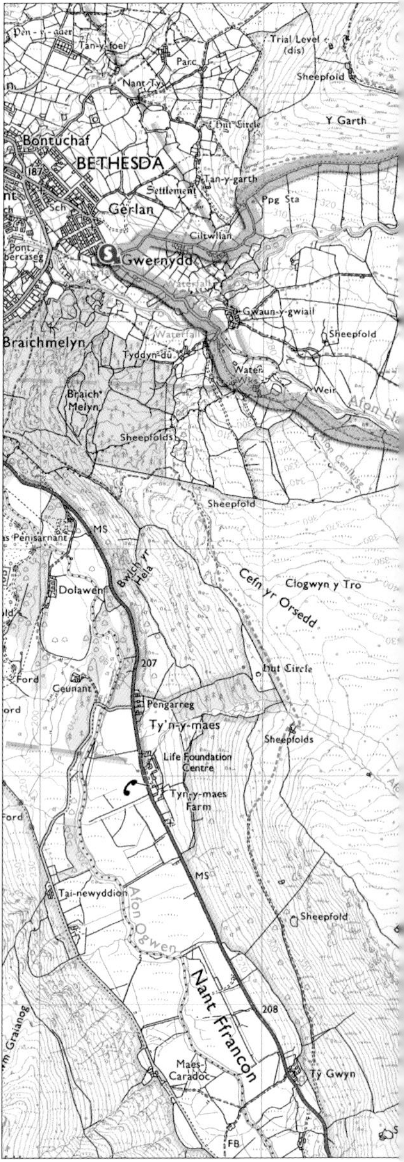
Tan-y-foel
Parc
Nant-Ty
Trial Level (dis)
Sheepfold
Y Garth
Hut Circle
Bontuchaf
BETHESDA
187
Tan-y-garth
Settlement
Ppg Sta
Sch
Gerlan
Ciltwllan
Gwernydd
Waterfall
Gwaun-y-gwiail
Sheepfold
Braichmelyn
Tyddyn-dû
Water Wks
Weir
Braich Melyn
Sheepfolds
Afon Llafar
Afon Gerenig
Sheepfold
MS
Penisarnant
Bwlch yr Hela
Cefn yr Orsedd
Clogwyn y Tro
Dolawen
207
Hut Circle
Ford
Ceunant
Pengarreg
Ty'n-y-maes
Sheepfolds
Life Foundation Centre
Tyn-y-maes Farm
MS
Tai-newyddion
Afon Ogwen
Sheepfold
Nant Ffrancon
208
Maes-Caradoc
Tŷ Gwyn
FB

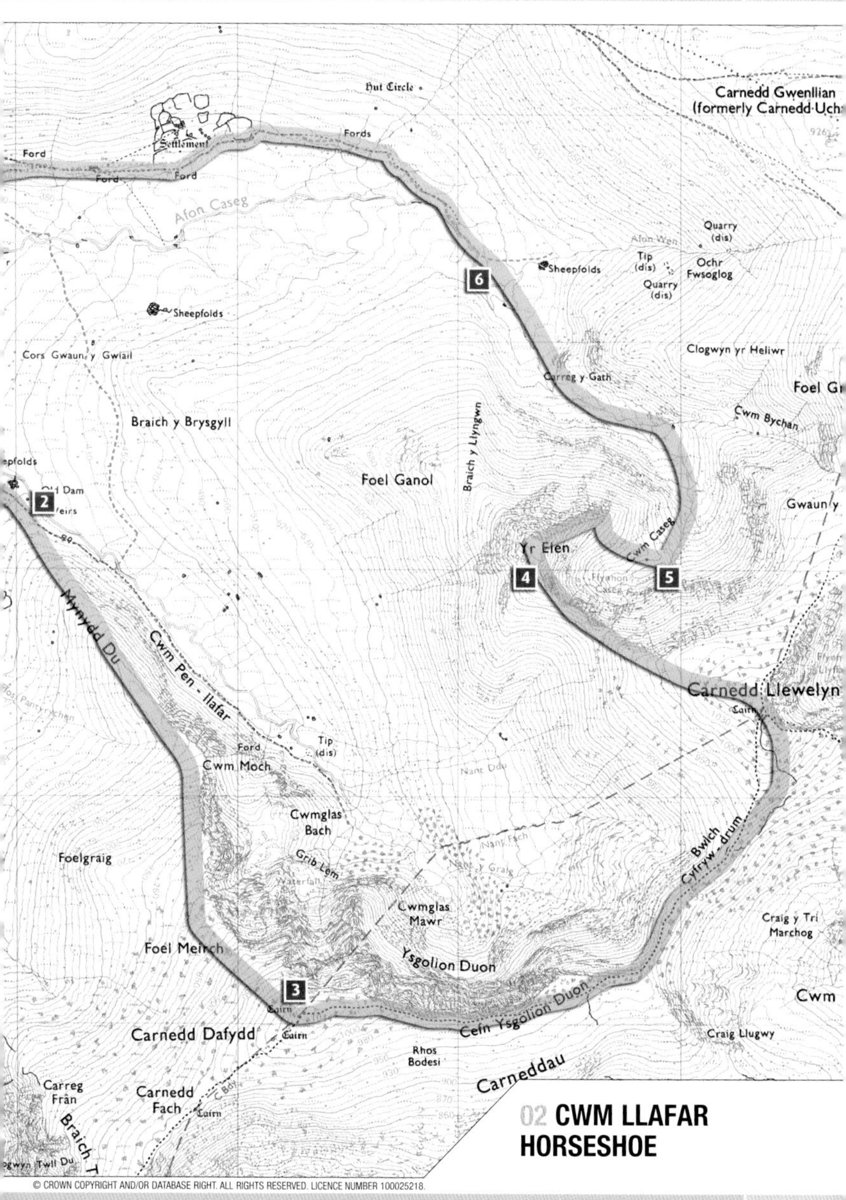

02 CWM LLAFAR HORSESHOE

Directions – Cwm Llafar Horseshoe

S Follow the narrow lane (Fford Gerlan) **south-east** out of the village and ignore another lane on the left – your return route – to continue to the end of the road, where you **bear left** past a waterworks sign. At the next gate (marked *Private*), **bear right** over a stile, and then **turn left** to follow the fence up to another stile. Cross this and **turn right**, now following spasmodic marker posts past some ruins and out onto open ground with the Afon Llafar now down to your left. Continue to an obvious fork above some sheepfolds.

2 **Bear right** and follow a faint path up over the grassy top of Mynydd Du and on to the rockier summit of Moel Meirch. The direct line involves a small amount of re-ascent, but it is possible to trace faint paths around the southern slopes of both tops if you'd prefer to save the energy. From Moel Meirch, a short, sharp and stony climb leads onto the 1,044m summit of Carnedd Dafydd.

3 **Bear left** to continue eastwards above the Black Ladders (Ysgolion Duon) and then veer **north-east** to climb steeply to the summit plateau of Carnedd Llewelyn. To descend, head **north-west** and then **west** to drop into a deep notch before climbing the outlying summit of Yr Elen by its pleasant, pinnacled, south-east ridge.

4 From the main top, head for the slightly lower northern top, and then drop down the sharp north-east ridge, either continuing all the way to the Afon Caseg, or breaking off near the bottom to visit the shores of the lovely Ffynnon Caseg.

5 Once at the head of the stream, follow faint paths along the true right-hand bank (water to your left), and after a vague, steep initial section you should be able to pick up a clearer track that contours around the hillside, staying high above the boggiest ground. Follow this to a ford of the Afon Wen.

6 Here a much better track establishes itself and continues down the valley, eventually funnelling you through a gate and onto a walled track. Follow this down to the road head, close to the pumping station, and then continue down to the fork in Gerlan, where you **turn right** to return to where you started.

PEN YR OLE WEN FROM FFYNNON LLOER

03 The Southern Carneddau

16km/10miles

Airy walking and easy scrambling combine to make one of Snowdonia's finest outings

Llyn Ogwen » Cwm Lloer » Pen yr Ole Wen (978m) » Carnedd Dafydd (1,044m) » Carnedd Llewelyn (1,064m) » Pen yr Helgi Du (833m) » Y Braich » Llyn Ogwen

Start

Ample parking anywhere along the A5 close to the eastern tip of Llyn Ogwen. GR: SH 667604.

The Walk

The ridges of the Southern Carneddau are among the most spectacular in the national park – narrow enough to feel airy and slightly daring, yet broad enough to stride out and enjoy. Enchained, they make one of the best mountain days Snowdonia can offer. They also make a fine introduction to the more 'hands on' style of walking/easy scrambling more usually associated with the nearby Glyderau.

The walk starts by climbing up to the hidden gem of Cwm Lloer – a stunning secluded cirque cut into the rugged flanks of Pen yr Ole Wen. From the floor of this magical spot, it climbs steeply via some easy scrambling, onto the mountain's east ridge, a broad boulder spur that sets the tone for most of the circuit.

Next up comes Carnedd Dafydd, at 1,044m, the range's number two, and a fine mountain at that. And from its cairned summit, there's a pleasant drop into Bwlch Cyfrwy-drum, via the airy walkway of Cefn Ysgolion Duon.

It's another rocky horror show on the final pull up onto Carnedd Llewelyn (1,064m), but the views make it worthwhile, and there's plenty of shelter around if you need a breather. Then it's down again, this time via a slender spur that leads into the saddle of Bwlch Eryl Farchog. There are a few hands-on moves along the way, and a few more on the clamber up to Pen yr Helgi Du. But from here, the descent starts in earnest.

The soft grass of Y Braich offers welcome respite for tired feet as you plummet back into the Ogwen Valley via a real pot-pourri of paths and tracks. And the views south to the Glyderau and Snowdon Massifs provide plenty of distraction should you need it.

THE SOUTHERN CARNEDDAU

DISTANCE: 16KM/10MILES » **TOTAL ASCENT:** 1,170M/3,838FT » **START GR:** SH 667604 » **TIME:** 6–7 HOURS **MAP:** OS EXPLORER OL17 SNOWDON » **REFRESHMENTS:** CAFÉ AT IDWAL COTTAGE, OR THE PINNACLE CAFÉ OR THE BRYN TYRCH INN IN CAPEL CURIG » **TRANSPORT:** BUSES BETWEEN THE OGWEN VALLEY AND CAPEL CURIG » **NAVIGATION:** STRAIGHTFORWARD ON CLEAR PATHS FOR THE MOST PART BUT CARE MUST BE TAKEN TO LOCATE THE BEST SCRAMBLING LINES.

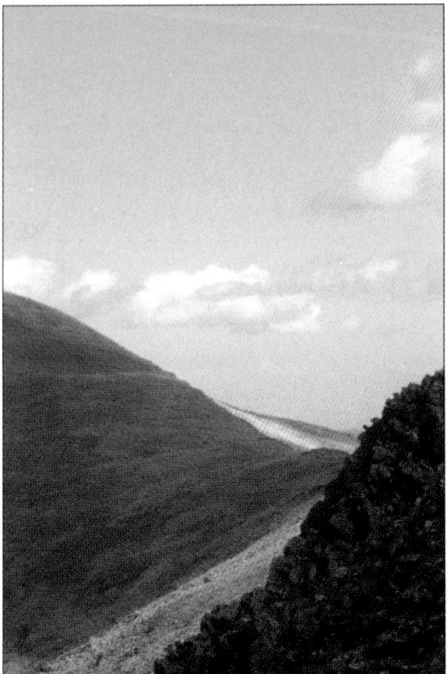

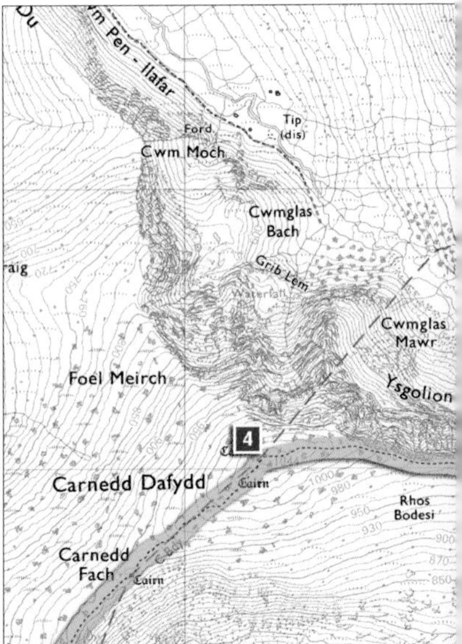

Ford
Tip (dis)
Cwm Moch
Cwmglas Bach
Grib Lem
Cwmglas Mawr
Foel Meirch
Ysgolion
4
Carnedd Dafydd
Cairn
Rhos Bodesi
Carnedd Fach
Cairn
Cwm Lloer
Bryn Mawr
Ford
Clogwyn Mawr
3
Pen yr Ole Wen
Ford
Yr Ole Wen
Ford
2
FB
Tal y Llyn Ogwen
Ford
Ford
Ford
Glan Dena
66
Llyn Ogwen
P
306
Milestone Buttress
Creigiau'r Dena

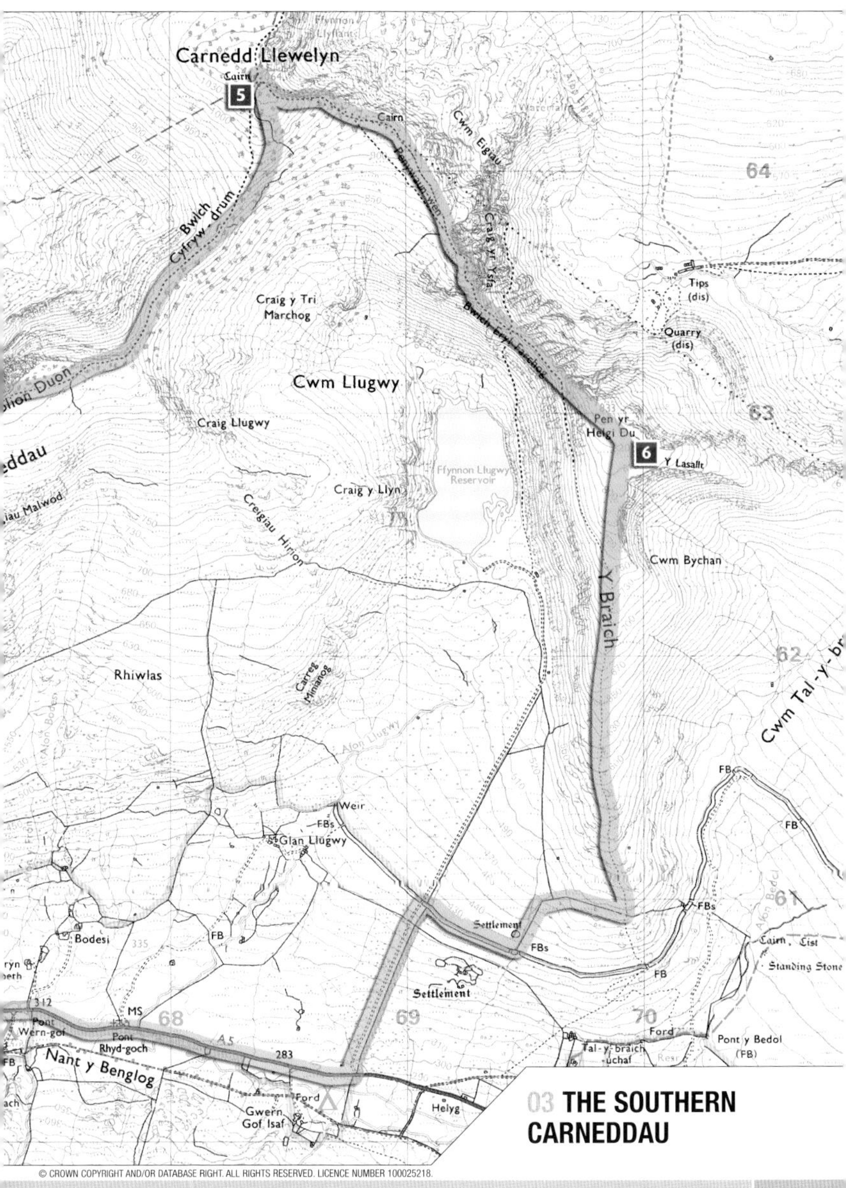

03 THE SOUTHERN CARNEDDAU

Directions – The Southern Carneddau

S Leave the A5 at the eastern end of Llyn Ogwen, where you should follow the drive that runs north past Glan Dena. Continue towards Tal y Llyn Ogwen Farm, but as the drive swings left into the farmyard, keep **straight ahead** onto a footpath that climbs alongside a dry stone wall to a stile. Cross this and continue to a marker post, where you should **turn right** to head directly uphill towards Cwm Lloer.

2 Stay with marker posts to a gap in a wall and then continue up, **half right**, with the Afon Lloer down to your right. As you enter the cwm, head half left to cross some boggy ground to the foot of the eastern spur of Pen yr Ole Wen, where a short gully provides the first of a number of easy scrambles.

3 Continue above the gully, keeping the steep escarpment to your right, and you'll wind easily up the ridge, eventually topping-out just a few metres short of Pen yr Ole Wen's 978m summit. Now turn **northwards** to follow a clear path down into Bwlch yr Ole Wen, with the steep headwall of Cwm Lloer down to your right. Pass a huge ancient cairn and drop into a tiny niche, before climbing again to a larger cairn atop Carnedd Dafydd.

4 Continue **eastwards** to follow the cliff edge along; now with the Black Ladders – a renowned winter climbing spot – down to your left. At Bwlch Cyfrwy-drum an obvious stony track leads up a final rock-strewn slope to the summit of Carnedd Llewelyn, where there's a choice of cairns and shelters, as well as some fine views.

5 To descend, leave the mountain to the **south-east**, following a clear path down above steep cliffs, where you'll see Ffynnon Llyfant – Wales's highest lake – far below. **Keep right** at a fork, and continue easily down onto the spur of Penywaun Wen. **Keep ahead** and scramble easily down into Bwlch Eryl Farchog, which is another delightfully airy ridge, and then continue to the foot of the steep north-western flank of Pen yr Helgi Du, where another short, sharp scramble gains the summit.

6 **Turn right** and follow a clear path down the long grassy spur of Y Braich. Drop steeply to a gap in a wall and then **bear diagonally right** to cross a pasture and drop to a footbridge over a narrow leat. Cross this and **bear right** to trace its path around the hillside to the Ffynnon Llugwy access road. **Bear left** onto this and follow it easily down to the A5, where you should **turn right** to return to the start.

THE SUMMIT PLATEAU OF CARNEDD LLEWELYN IN FULL WINTER CONDITIONS

LLYN CRAFNANT FROM NEAR CRIMPIAU

04 The Eastern Carneddau

12km/7.5miles

A lonely walk over remote modest-sized peaks with fine views

Llyn Crafnant » Creigiau Gleision (634m) » Craig Wen » Crimpiau » Llyn Crafnant

Start

Forestry Commission car park near Llyn Crafnant. This is reached by following narrow lanes south-west from the B5106 at Trefriw. GR: SH 755617

The Walk

The best views are never seen from the stage itself. In fact, sometimes they are better from the rear of the hall where the whole spectacle can be witnessed in one frame. This is definitely true of the Ogwen Valley where the high peaks of the Glyderau and the Carneddau crowd tightly around Llyn Ogwen making it almost impossible to appreciate their full grandeur.

It's a show that's definitely at its most impressive from the east, where the distinctive shape of Tryfan stands tall and bold against a panoramic backdrop of Y Garn and the two main Glyderau summits. And the best seats are on the summits of Creigiau Gleision and Crimpiau, at the far eastern edge of the Carneddau range. At 634m, the Creigiau Gleision is barely half the height of its parent peak – the mighty Carnedd Llewelyn. But don't be misled: size isn't everything, and the walking in this little-known corner of the national park is as enthralling as anywhere. Perhaps more so because it never sees the crowds.

The walk starts at the beauty spot of Llyn Crafnant – a narrow, shimmering waterway surrounded by forestry. But it soon climbs above the trees to strike out along an exhilarating ridge, with the views improving with almost every step. From the high point, the paths get fainter, and the ground more complex, but you should be in your stride by now, and hopefully savouring every step.

Crimpiau may seem like one climb too many from the col beneath it, but the remote, rock-topped summit is a delight and definitely worth the entry fee.

This isn't a long walk, and it doesn't gain that much height either; but it does cross a lot of rough ground on paths that aren't always easy to follow and for that reason, it's definitely best not underestimated.

THE EASTERN CARNEDDAU

DISTANCE: 12KM/7.5MILES » **TOTAL ASCENT:** 790M/2,591FT » **START GR:** SH 755617 » **TIME:** 5–6 HOURS
MAP: OS EXPLORER OL17 SNOWDON » **REFRESHMENTS:** CAFÉ BY LLYN CRAFNANT » **TRANSPORT:** NONE » **NAVIGATION:** SOME CLEAR TRACKS AND PATHS BUT SOME TRACKLESS GROUND AND SOME SECTIONS THAT WOULD BE AWKWARD IN POOR VISIBILITY.

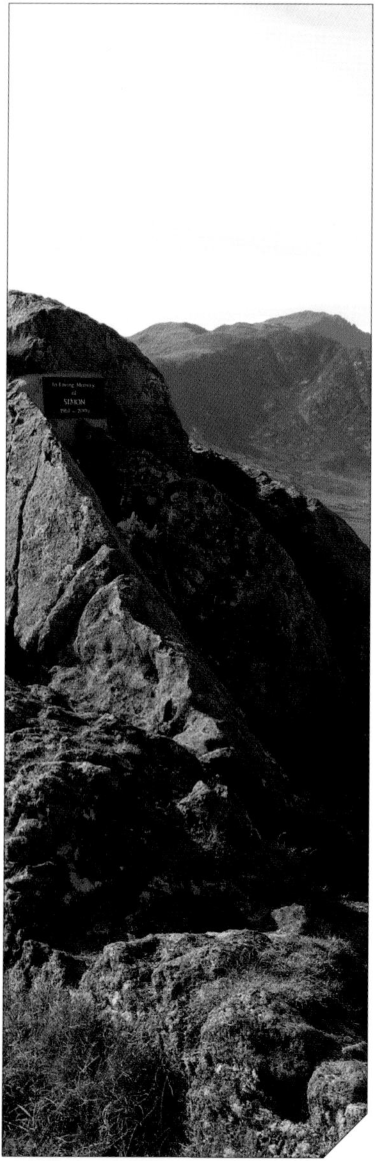

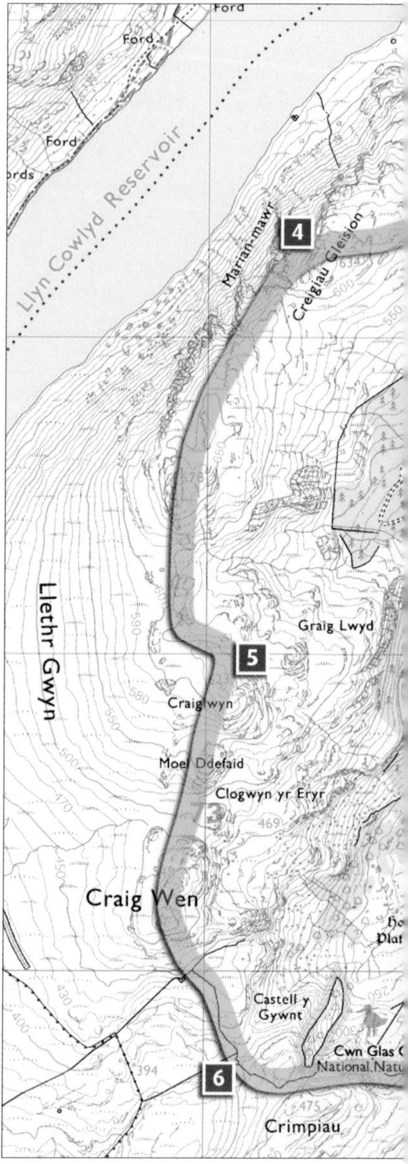

Ford
Ford
Ford
Llyn Cowlyd Reservoir
Marian-mawr
Creigiau Gleision
634
600
550
650
678
4
Llethr Gwyn
Graig Lwyd
5
590
580
Craig-lwyn
550
500
Moel Ddefaid
Clogwyn yr Eryr
469
470
450
Craig Wen
430
400
Castell y Gwynt
394
6
Cwn Glas
475
Crimpiau

04 THE EASTERN CARNEDDAU

Directions – The Eastern Carneddau

S Walk back out the car park and **turn left** to walk back down the road for nearly a kilometre. **Turn left** onto a broad tarmac track, opposite a house, and follow this up and around a left-hand bend to continue past a drive, where it becomes a rough track. Follow it around to the right and then left and then right again, where another drive goes straight on. And then continue around to the **left** before heading up to a stile. Cross this and continue up through hazel trees to join a broad track.

2 **Turn left** and follow this as it winds its ever narrowing way upwards. Continue to a stile in a corner where fences meet. Cross this and **keep ahead** for 200m before **bearing left** to cross another stile onto a clear but narrow path. Follow this as it dips then swings **slightly right** to rejoin the fence a few hundred metres further on. Cross the next stile and **turn left** to continue uphill with the fence to your left.

3 Continue onto the crest of the ridge and then **bear left** over another ladder stile to follow a clear path to the first of Creigiau Gleision's summits, which offers magnificent views over the Cowlyd Reservoir to the main summits of the Carneddau as well as Tryfan, Y Garn and the Glyderau.

4 **Keep ahead** to drop past a broad band of quartz and then continue, mainly on a clear path, until you reach the mountain's main top, marked with a cairn. **Keep ahead** again to drop very steeply down onto the broad plateau below the peak and then continue in the same direction, crossing a boggy area and then climbing to the top of Craiglwyn.

5 Drop steeply from this and now stay with the path as it skirts to the west of the rocky knolls of Moel Ddefaid and Craig Wen. Drop from the latter down to a gap in the wall and follow the path through another gap and eventually down into a deep col beneath Crimpiau.

6 Climb slightly to the **right** to follow a clear path to the summit of *Crimpiau*, which must be one of Snowdonia's finest viewpoints. Continue **straight ahead** to drop down to the next col, with good views now over Llyn Crafnant to the north, and **turn left** onto the main path to follow it down through a gate into a field. Keep to the **right-hand** path to drop to a lane at a crossroads.

7 Go **straight across** to walk past a wooden chalet and a large house and then go through a gate where the path leads over a footbridge on the right. Take this and follow it upwards to join a broad forest path. **Turn right** onto this and follow it easily back around Llyn Crafnant to the road. **Turn left** to return to the car park.

CREIGAU GLEISION WITH THE OGWEN VALLEY AND Y GLYDERAU AS A BACKDROP

STILE IN CWM TRYFAN

05 Y Glyderau

10km/6miles

A hands-free tour of the mighty peaks of the Glyderau

Idwal Cottage » Bwlch Tryfan » Glyder Fach (994m) » Glyder Fawr (1001m) » Devil's Kitchen » Llyn Idwal

Start

Main car park at Idwal Cottage, on the A5 at the western end of Llyn Ogwen. Easiest reached by the A5 west from Betws-y-Coed. GR: SH 649604.

The Walk

The northern slopes of the rock-strewn Glyderau appear almost impenetrable from the glacier-gouged cwms below. But there are weaknesses. To the east of the peaks a rough path straddles Bwlch Tryfan before joining an old miner's path to cut an airy line around the head of the cwm of the same name – perfect for an easy ascent of Glyder Fach. And west of Glyder Fawr, the infamous Devil's Kitchen path weaves an unlikely line down the steep, bouldery hillside. Linking the two together brings the two main peaks, and the sumptuous scenery of their deeply cloven northern cwms, within reach of walkers that prefer not to use their hands.

But this doesn't make it a cinch either: the boulder-hopping ascent to the shores of Llyn Bochlwyd, sometimes known as Australia Lake due to its shape, sets the tone well. And the rubble-strewn path from the lake to the stile in Bwlch Tryfan continues in a similar vein. There's height to be squandered once in Cwm Tryfan – painful after all that climbing – and then another stiff ascent onto the main ridge as well. And even then the steep stuff's not totally despatched: there's still quite a pull up to Glyder Fach.

From here, it is a little easier though; although the rough nature of the ground remains the same. The Cantilever Stone is the main attraction on Glyder Fach – photo stop obligatory – but perhaps the most eye-catching feature of the whole ridge is the jagged turrets of Castell y Gwynt – the Castle of the Winds – a true rock icon if ever there was one.

Glyder Fawr seems a cheerier place since its recent promotion to the 1,000m club, and its summit rocks offer almost endless opportunities for shelter and a spot of lunch. The descent to Llyn y Cwn is still as brutal as ever though; and the slabby steps of the Kitchen path are pretty unforgiving on already aching knees.

Y GLYDERAU

DISTANCE: 10KM/6MILES » **TOTAL ASCENT:** 900M/2,952FT » **START GR:** SH 649604 » **TIME:** 5-6 HOURS **MAP:** OS EXPLORER OL17 SNOWDON » **REFRESHMENTS:** TEA & SNACKS IN THE CAR PARK » **TRANSPORT:** BUSES SERVE THE OGWEN VALLEY FROM CAPEL CURIG » **NAVIGATION:** TRACKS ARE GENERALLY CLEAR AND WELL-CAIRNED, BUT THE TOPS AREN'T MUCH FUN IN POOR VISIBILITY.

Directions – Y Glyderau

S Leave the car park by walking past the toilet block and follow the well-surfaced Cwm Idwal path over the bridge and up to a sharp right-hand bend. Leave the main track here, and continue **straight ahead**, still on a clear path, towards the banks of the Nant Bochlwyd. The path then climbs steeply over jumbled boulders to the outflow of Llyn Bochlwyd.

2 Continue past the lake and follow a rough path into the very obvious dip of Bwlch Tryfan, directly ahead. Cross a ladder stile that vaults a wall in the centre of the col and then keep **straight ahead** to drop slightly into Cwm Tryfan. Keep **straight ahead** the whole time and you'll be able to make out the continuation path that tracks around the head of the cwm and then climbs diagonally up onto the ridge. This is the Miner's Track and following it from Cwm Tryfan will provide a relatively easy, hands-free route onto the main Glyderau ridge.

3 Once on the ridge, **turn right** onto a vague track, that quickly establishes itself, and follow it up towards Glyder Fach. This steepens and becomes quite rough for a bit, before finally easing again and leading past the distinctive Cantilever Stone to the rocky blocks that mark the summit.

4 Now **head west** to the dramatic turrets of Castell y Gwynt, and drop leftwards into Bwlch y Ddwy-Glyder (**note**: any attempt to do this more directly results in awkward boulder-hopping). At the bottom, trend **rightwards**, deep into the niche, and then follow the path back out.

5 This splits with the higher, right-hand track hugging the escarpment edge, with all the associated views, while the lower one makes a beeline for the 1,001m summit of Glyder Fawr. Either will do the job.

6 Leave the summit to the **west** on a cairned path, and then veer **north-west** to descend steeply and relentlessly to Llyn y Cwn (Lake of the Dogs), which sits in a deep col above the infamous Devil's Kitchen.

7 **Bear right** on the clear path and follow it between sinister-looking rock walls, where steep steps take over. Continue down to a junction of paths and **bear right** to drop further before finally branching out across the hillside.

8 Cross the Idwal Stream, and pass beneath the Idwal Slabs – a popular climbing area – before following a clear path along the shores of Llyn Idwal. **Keep ahead** through a gate and follow the main path back to Idwal Cottage.

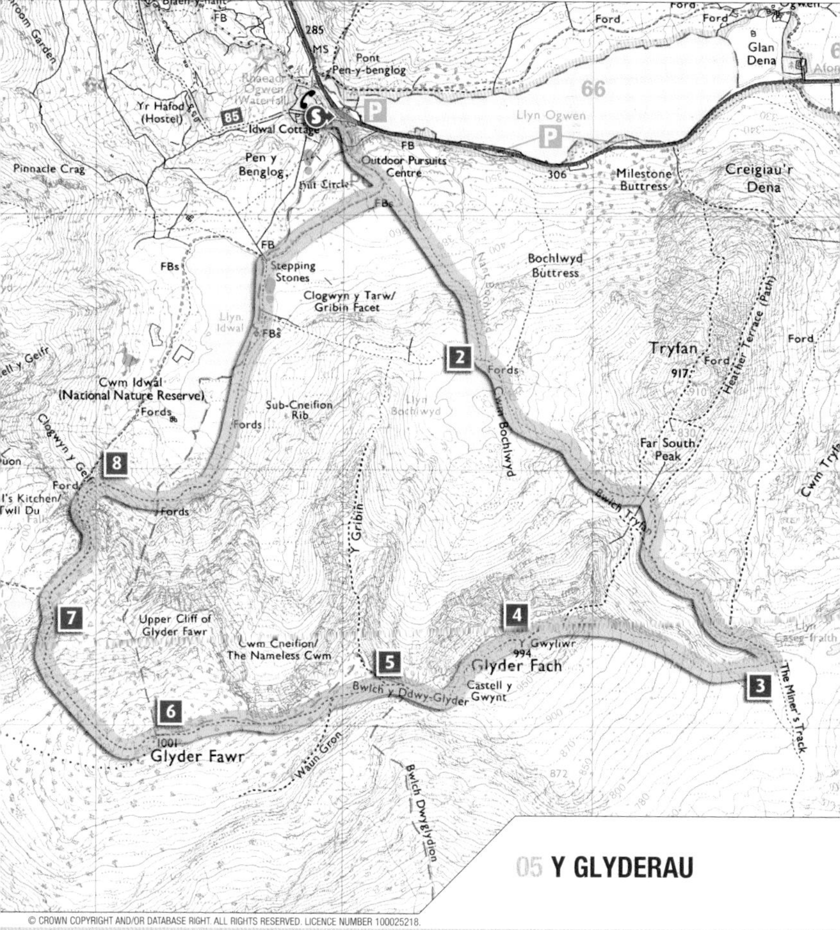

05 Y GLYDERAU

THE CANTILEVER STONE ON GLYDER FACH

06 **Glyder Fawr** from the **South** 10.5km/6.5miles

An almost gentle route to the top of the iconic Glyder

Pen y Gwryd » Pen-y-Pass » Glyder Fawr (1,001m) » Glyder Fach (994m) » Pen y Gwryd

Start

Parking near the Pen y Gwryd Hotel, on the A498, south of Capel Curig. GR: SH 660557.

The Walk

The Glyderau ridge is notoriously rocky. In fact the northern slopes are home to some of Wales's finest rock climbs. But the southern flanks of the ridge are a different matter altogether with the rocky bristles that define the massif dissolving into steep grassy slopes that offer a very different walking experience.

This walk can be started from Pen-y-Pass but the car park here usually fills quicker than those down the hill, and this also involves a steep pull back uphill from the Pen y Gwryd Hotel at the very end - never very pleasant.

So the description starts down on the valley floor, where a brand new path leads painlessly up to the Youth Hostel. A good path takes over, and offers fine views in all directions, especially across to Crib Goch (p123), which is particularly striking from this angle, and down over the Llanberis Pass.

The grassy path snakes ever upwards between outcrops finding seemingly easy ways through or around the kind of ground that at first appears impassable. It finally levels just a short distance from the summit.

The next section covers the same ground as Walk 5 in reverse. First down to Bwlch y Ddwy Glyder, and then around the atmospheric turrets of Castell y Gwynt and up to Glyder Fach. The descent from here carries this theme further, dropping you onto easier ground close to Llyn y Caseg-fraith, where you pick up the continuation of the Miner's Path taken by the previous walk.

This then drops south onto seldom-trod ground with great views over Moel Siabod and the main Moelwynion ridge. The final section trudges easily over soft ground delivering you back to the A498, close to the hotel. At this stage you'll be glad you started at the bottom.

GLYDER FAWR FROM THE SOUTH

DISTANCE: 10.5KM/6.5MILES » **TOTAL ASCENT:** 870M/2,854FT » **START GR:** SH 660557 » **TIME:** 5-6 HOURS **MAP:** OS EXPLORER OL17 SNOWDON » **REFRESHMENTS:** CAFÉ AT PEN-Y-PASS AND BAR IN THE PEN Y GWRYD HOTEL **TRANSPORT:** PEN-Y-PASS IS THE MAIN BUS TERMINAL SO CAN BE REACHED FROM PRETTY MUCH ANYWHERE » **NAVIGATION:** MAINLY CLEAR TRACKS AND PATHS BUT SOME SECTIONS WOULD BE AWKWARD IN POOR VISIBILITY.

Directions – Glyder Fawr from the South

S Start by locating the new, well-signed path that leads **west** from just south of the Llanberis Pass road. Take this and follow it easily up to Pen-y-Pass where you need to cross the road and locate a path that starts to the left of the Youth Hostel. This goes through a gate and across a garden to access the open hillside.

2 Now follow an obvious path steeply upwards until the gradient eases where you **bear left** to continue easily until you see Llyn Cwmffynnon down to your right. Drop to cross a boggy col and then climb again, this time onto the south ridge proper.

3 The path is vague in places, but if you keep **straight ahead** you'll eventually find yourself on an exposed terrace high above the Llanberis Pass, with the impressive north face of Crib Goch facing you across the valley. Steeper ground leads back onto the crest of the ridge, where the path, now daubed with blobs of red paint, weaves its way through a number of outcrops, eventually emerging onto easier ground. Continue past clusters of fallen flakes to the trig point, which is hidden among boulders.

4 To descend, **head east**, following a well-cairned path to the edge of the escarpment above Cwm Cneifion. From here, continue down into Bwlch y Ddwy Glyder, with great views over the Ogwen Valley and the Carneddau massif.

5 Stay with the path, which drops to the right before winding left again through a mass of jumbled boulders to the pinnacled turrets of Castell y Gwynt (Castle of the Wind). A clear path now leads north-east from here to the 994m (3,261ft) summit of Glyder Fach.

6 Continue in the same direction to the top of Bristly Ridge - identified by cairns and some more spiky pinnacles - and then **keep right**, to stay high, following a faint path that continues eastwards down a steep, boulder-covered slope. This eventually relents and a clear path leads onto a plateau. **Keep ahead** until you see a small cairn, which marks the junction with the Miner's Track, coming up from Cwm Tryfan.

7 **Bear right**, to cross the saddle, as if aiming for the lowest point. The path is vague in places as it reaches the far side, but keep **straight ahead** (south) - to the right of a large rocky knoll - and it soon establishes itself again.

8 Now follow the obvious stony track downwards, passing some wonderful waterfalls along the way. Ford the stream and descend to a stile, before following the line of a dry stone wall across some very wet ground. Continue over the bridge over the Nant Gwryd and then **keep ahead** to join the road close to the hotel.

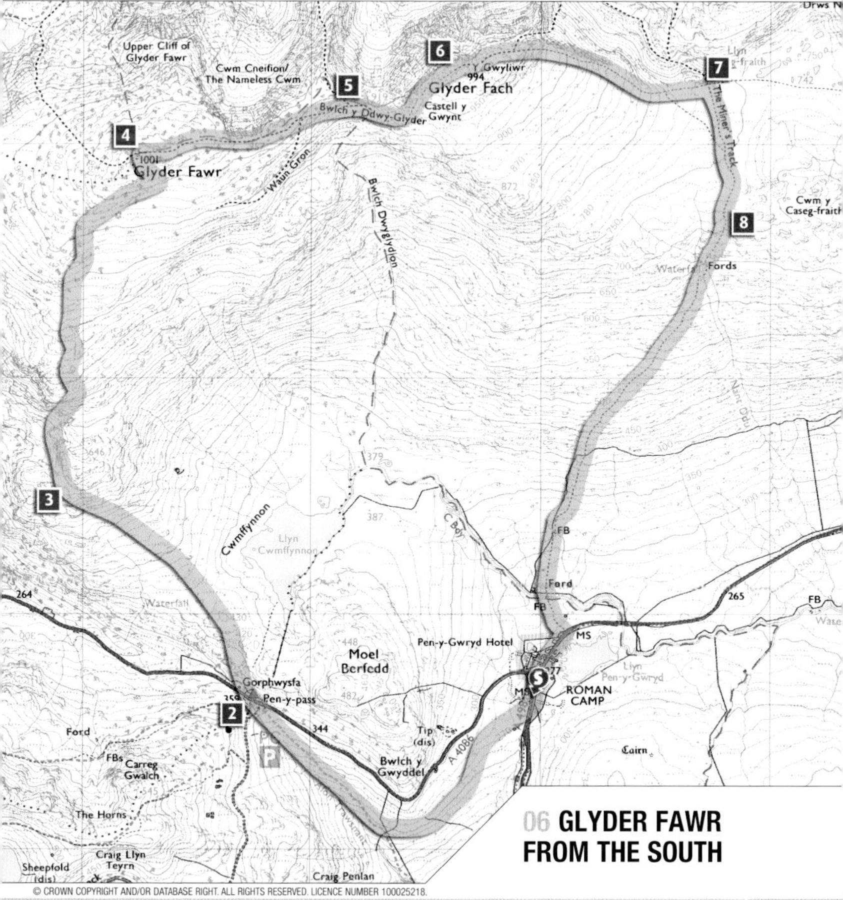

06 GLYDER FAWR FROM THE SOUTH

ELIDIR FACH FROM MARCHLYN BACH

07 Elidir Fawr from the West

16km/10miles

Varied walking to the top of Y Glyderau's least climbed 3000-footer

Deiniolen » Carnedd y Filiast (821m) » Mynydd Perfedd (812m) » Elidir Fawr (924m) » Elidir Fach (795m) » Deiniolen

Start

Park at the road head above Deiniolen (east of the village) GR: SH 596630.

The Walk

It's the one everybody forgets; the outlying Glyder that doesn't tie easily in with the main cluster of Ogwen peaks; and the one that calls for the lengthy out-and-back detour when completing the Welsh 3,000's. And if this isn't reason enough to give Snowdonia's number 15 a wide berth, take a look at its eastern flanks: desecrated by years of slate mining; or take a tour of the Electric Mountain to visit a huge power station concealed deep within its bowels.

But somehow Elidir Fawr rises above all this – metaphorically as well as physically – and it is still a stunning mountain with an impressive rugged profile from almost any perspective. It also has enough rock on its slender summit ridge to make it feel every bit as wild as its nearby cousins.

It's also a viewpoint extraordinaire, with stunning vistas east across Cwm Ffrancon to the main peaks of the Carneddau; and even more far-reaching panoramas south, to Snowdon, the Nantlle Hills and, on a good day, even the distant Yr Eifl peaks of the Llyn Peninsula. It's probably fair to say that Elidir Fawr looks and feels better from its summit than it does when standing beneath.

This is a walk for the Snowdonia connoisseur: the intrepid explorer that can take the mountains of North Wales warts and all. It starts by easily following the rather intrusive Marchlyn Dam access road across barren wasteland. You might wonder what you're letting yourself in for. But as the views improve, the rubble is forgotten. And by the time you reach Carnedd y Filliast and gaze across the chasm beyond to the shapely lines of the main act you'll be than happy you made the effort. It only gets better from here.

ELIDIR FAWR FROM THE WEST

DISTANCE: 16KM/10MILES » **TOTAL ASCENT:** 680M/2,230FT » **START GR:** SH 596630 » **TIME:** 4-5 HOURS
MAP: OS EXPLORER OL17 SNOWDON » **REFRESHMENTS:** Y CABAN IN BRYNREFAIL IS THE BEST BET » **TRANSPORT:** NONE
NAVIGATION: MAINLY CLEAR PATHS THOUGH SOME SECTIONS WOULD BE TOUGH IN POOR VISIBILITY.

Directions – Elidir Fawr from the West

S Go through the gate and head up the access road past a disused quarry on the right. Continue to a fork, where you can scramble up a bank to get a look at Marchlyn Bach, and then **keep ahead**, on the main track, with the reservoir now to your right.

2 Leave the track to the **left** – about 100m before a sharp right-hand bend – and keep the fence to your left to cross boggy ground to a stream. Ford this and **bear right** to follow the wall upwards on a vague path. This leads back onto the access road briefly.

3 Continue for 100m and you'll see a stile on your left. Cross this and follow the obvious path up to the saddle beneath Carnedd y Filliast. **Bear right** at a small pool, and climb the ridge directly, keeping to the left as much as possible for great views over the Carneddau.

4 The rocky top of Carnedd y Filliast comes as something of a surprise after the grassy slopes of the ascent but there's a good windbreak on the top, if you fancy a rest. Drop down off the rocky ridge, and follow the line of it **southwards**, crossing open ground and eventually coming to a stile. Cross this – great views south-east towards Tryfan – and continue in the same direction to a shelter on the flat top of Mynydd Perfedd.

5 Bear **slightly right** here and drop down into Bwlch y Marchlyn, following the narrowing ridge as closely as you can. You'll meet a path coming up from Bwlch y Brecan, which you can now follow steeply upwards to Elidir Fawr's slender rock-strewn summit ridge. A cairn and windbreak mark the top.

6 Continue along the ridge, treading your way carefully through the jumble of boulders, until you drop into a deep notch. Look right here and you should make out a faint path dropping down through the scree towards the small cairn that marks the summit of Elidir Fach. Make your way down the steep slope and cross easy ground to the cairn.

7 **Bear right** here and follow a faint path **northwards** until you reach the steep escarpment edge. The path at this stage actually follows the national park boundary. Now drop steeply down, with the edge to your right, staying with the path and aiming at the northern tip of the reservoir. You'll meet a wall that will take you the last few metres to the road. **Turn left** onto the road and retrace your earlier tracks back to the road head.

07 ELIDIR FAWR FROM THE WEST

SNOWDON FROM LLYNNAU MYMBYR

08 **Snowdon** by **The Pyg Track** 12km/7miles

A strenuous but straightforward ramble from Snowdon's most scenic side

Pen-y-pass » Bwlch y Moch » Snowdon (1,085m) » Llyn Llydaw » Pen-y-pass

Start

There's a large car park at Pen-y-pass but it fills very quickly – arrive early at busy times. GR: SH 647556.

The Walk

The true trade route up Snowdon (Yr Wyddfa in Welsh) follows the railway line from Llanberis. It's perhaps the easiest route, and almost certainly the most straightforward, but it's also stingy on views, especially of the mountain itself, and devoid of atmosphere. This route, however, has both in abundance and is therefore a far better way for inexperienced walkers to make a summit bid on Wales's highest peak.

The Pyg Track kicks off by escaping the main cwm altogether and sneaking around the steep hillside that drops into the Llanberis Pass. But at Bwlch y Moch – the Pass of the Pigs – it finally vaults the eastern walls at the foot of Crib Goch and then dips slightly before turning right to strike a direct line across the mountain's western flanks.

The views are truly wonderful. Snowdon is at its very best from this perspective and the lake-jewelled cwm makes an impressive foreground. It's also a great opportunity to view the steep walls of Y Lliwedd on the other side of the valley. This is the home of the longest rock climbs in Wales and it really does resemble a mini Eigerwand from here.

The Pyg Track and the Miner's Track join forces as the going gets steeper. And from here they march on relentlessly with fine views over Snowdon's Trinity Face. The final zigzag signals impending relief and at Bwlch Glas the gradient eases enough for breath to be regained.

From here, all the paths on this side of the mountain meet. And there'll be no shortage of companionship for the final few paces. The summit can be disappointing, especially if it's crammed full with railway passengers. But a little exploration always reveals a quiet spot, and then there's the smug satisfaction of knowing you got there the hard way.

SNOWDON BY THE PYG TRACK

DISTANCE: 12KM/7MILES » **TOTAL ASCENT:** 900M/2,952FT » **START GR:** SH 647556 » **TIME:** 6–7 HOURS **MAP:** OS EXPLORER OL17 SNOWDON » **REFRESHMENTS:** CAFE IN THE CAR PARK AND ON THE SUMMIT (IF YOU MUST) » **TRANSPORT:** PEN Y PASS IS THE MAIN BUS TERMINAL SO CAN BE EASILY REACHED » **NAVIGATION:** TRACKS ARE GENERALLY CLEAR AND EASY TO FOLLOW. **WARNING: IF THE MOUNTAIN IS COVERED IN SNOW, THIS ROUTE BECOMES A MOUNTAINEERING CHALLENGE NOT A WALK.**

Directions – Snowdon by The Pyg Track

S With your back to the road, head to the **right-hand** end of the car park where a clear, signed path leads out onto open ground. This is the Pyg Track. Now follow this until it eventually reaches the deep saddle beneath the obvious, sharp nose of Crib Goch (a path leads right to this).

2 **Don't** head towards Crib Goch but **keep ahead** to drop slightly and then follow the path as it tracks around the steep hillside with great views. Stay with this until it reaches steeper ground, where it joins the Miner's Track coming up from the lake below.

3 Now climb relentlessly upwards, eventually reaching a sharp switchback before finally cresting the ridge at Bwlch Glas. Here you join the main path coming up from Llanberis. **Bear left** and follow this steadily upwards to the cafe and the summit.

4 To descend, retrace your steps all the way back to the steep section where the two paths met earlier. **Now keep right** – down – to continue descending steeply to the shores of the Glaslyn lake.

5 Now simply follow the broad track as it winds down past Llyn Llydaw and around to the left to return to the car park.

SNOWDON AND LLYNNAU MYMBYR FROM CAPEL CURIG

08 SNOWDON BY THE PYG TRACK

SNOWDON AND THE SOUTH RIDGE FROM YR ARAN

09 Snowdon by the Watkin Path

13km/8miles

A true connoisseur's route to the summit of Wales

Bethania » Cwm Llan » Bwlch Ciliau » Snowdon (1,085m) » Bwlch Cwm Llan » Cwm Llan » Bethania

Start

Large pay and display car park at Bethania, between Beddgelert and Capel Curig. GR: SH 627506.

The Walk

Cwm Llan is an impressive valley: broad, steep-walled and cradling a spectacular tumbling stream. Its head is formed by an imposing bastion of craggy hillside that stretches from the lofty south face of Snowdon all the way across to the shapely outlier of Yr Aran. And the airy ridge that crowns this wall – usually referred to as Snowdon's south ridge – provides some fine walking.

The valley is explored by the opening section of this walk, which eases its way up broad mining tracks, eventually crossing the Afon Cwm Llan and passing the Gladstone Rock. This boasts a plaque commemorating a speech by then Prime Minister William Ewart Gladstone on the subject of Justice for Wales. It then continues past the remnants of long-closed slate quarries and mines before steepening and clambering breathlessly up to the pass of Bwlch Ciliau at the foot of Y Liwedd.

This offers wonderful views across the shimmering waters of Llyn Llydaw and Glaslyn, and above these the knife-edge ridge of Crib Goch and its loftier neighbour, Garnedd Ugain, dominate the skyline (p123). You'll also clearly see the Pyg Track and Miner's Track, both explored in Walk 08.

A good path now takes the ridge towards Snowdon, eventually dropping into Bwlch y Saethau at the foot of the mountain's south face. A steep scree field takes over here, and the next section, which leads onto the South Ridge, is the most arduous of the walk. The going eases once you're on the ridge, and the summit is not far above you now.

The descent follows the same route to start with. And most walkers will revel in the silence and solitude after the chaos of the cafe and train station at the top. But this time it continues all the way down into Bwlch Cwm Llan, where mixed paths drop you back to the valley floor.

SNOWDON BY THE WATKIN PATH

DISTANCE: 13KM/8MILES » **TOTAL ASCENT:** 1,140M/3,740FT » **START GR:** SH 627506 » **TIME:** 6–7 HOURS **MAP:** OS EXPLORER OL17 SNOWDON » **REFRESHMENTS:** CAFE GWYNANT, TOWARDS BEDDGELERT AND ON THE SUMMIT, OR PUBS IN BEDDGELERT » **TRANSPORT:** BUSES BETWEEN PEN Y PASS AND BEDDGELERT » **NAVIGATION:** TRACKS ARE GENERALLY CLEAR AND EASY TO FOLLOW BUT THE DESCENT FROM BWLCH CWM LLAN CAN BE COMPLICATED.

Directions – Snowdon by the Watkin Path

S Cross the road, **bear left** over the bridge and then **turn right** into the lane. Almost immediately bear left through a gate, marked *Watkin Path* and follow the path up into the trees, where you **turn right** to join a good track at a gate. **Turn left** and follow the track up into Cwm Llan, curving around to the left to enter the valley proper.

2 Stay with the main track as it swings left and right and go through a gate to carry on up past some fine waterfalls. The path climbs up above the falls, crossing an old quarry incline for a second time before passing beneath the broken crags of Clogwyn Brith and eventually dropping to the banks of the tumbling stream.

3 Cross the stream, and follow the path past the ruins of Plascwmllan: the remnants of a mansion that once housed the quarry bosses. Continue easily for a few minutes to the Gladstone Rock and then continue upwards around the craggy ridge of Craig-ddu into Cwm Tregalan, where you'll pass the roofless ruins of the old quarry barracks. Above here, the path turns **sharp right** and makes a steep ascent to Bwlch Ciliau.

4 The saddle opens up a whole new panorama, with wonderful views down over Glaslyn to the spiky walls of Crib Goch and of course the intimidating southern walls of Snowdon. **Turn left** to follow the path, or better still, the escarpment edge, over the top of Cribyn Ridge and down into Bwlch y Saethau.

5 The best and easiest way to the summit from here is to follow the main path **west** for a few hundred metres, with steep slopes above you to your right; and then to **bear right** onto an easier angled path that cuts up through the scree to a standing stone on the south ridge. (**Note**: attempts to short cut this make for hard work.) Once up, **bear right** onto the south ridge and follow a clear path up to the summit.

6 To descend, retrace your footsteps down to the standing stone and then continue along the ridge towards the Bwlch Cwm Llan, the deep col that divides Snowdon from Yr Aran. (An ascent of this peak could be added to the route but allow around an hour for the return trip). Once in the col, **turn left** to drop into upper Cwm Llan.

7 Follow the path steeply down to an old quarry track, which you **turn right** onto. Now follow this around the hillside and then steeply down an old incline to rejoin the track you walked earlier. **Turn right** onto this and retrace your steps back to the car park.

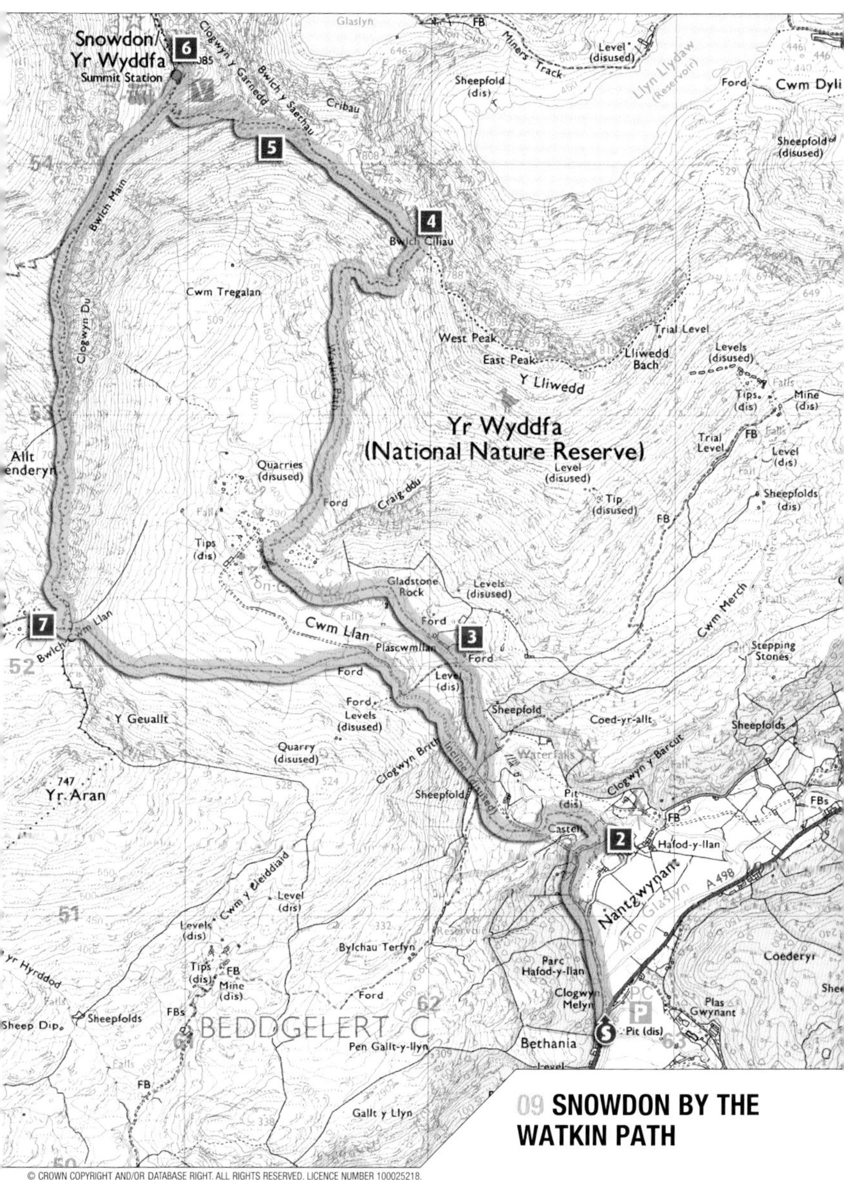

09 SNOWDON BY THE WATKIN PATH

SECTION 2

Central Snowdonia

What the central peaks lack in altitude, they more than make up for in wild and remote ambience. This is the place to find solitude in Snowdonia. Again there's plenty of variety: the Nantlle Ridge is special – a mix of rugged summits and easy scrambling, whereas the Moelwynion is a connoisseur's range really, with most of the drama at the northern and southern ends and a whole lot of nothing in between. The peaks of the Rhinogydd are inhospitable in places, but the steep and often rocky tops richly reward those prepared to make the effort.

RHINOG FACH FROM CWM NANTCOL

CWMORTHIN

NEAR THE SUMMIT OF CRAIG CWM SILYN

10 The Nantlle Ridge

10.5km/6miles

A lengthy linear ridge walk that takes some beating

Rhyd Ddu » Y Garn (633m) > Mynydd Drws-y-coed (695m) » Trum y Ddysgl (709m) Mynydd Tal-y-mignedd (653m) » Craig Cwm Silyn (734m) » Garnedd-goch (700m) » Maen Llwyd

Start

Large pay and display car park at Rhyd Ddu, on the A4085 between Beddgelert and Caernarfon. GR: SH 571525.

The Walk

The Nantlle Hills may lie just one valley over from Snowdon, but they somehow feel a whole world away, especially if you are lucky enough to experience them on a quieter day when it's possible to keep the airy walking and easy scrambling all to yourself. The pleasure can be added to by gazing east at the ants crawling all over the summit of the principality's tallest.

There's a definite elitism about these mountains. Just knowing about them implies a certain discern that the trainer-clad tourist is unlikely to understand; and making that first crossing is a kind of rite of passage that will put the aspiring hill walker off heavily-trod paths for life. Yet despite this air of mystery, the ridge is no more than a truly wonderful skyline walk, with a few easy scrambling sections thrown in to spice it up.

This is a linear walk so logistics come into play at the planning stage. The obvious solution is two cars and if you have these at your disposal then the route rolls out easily from east to west as described. Another alternative involves a local taxi firm, which has been operating along the ridge for some time, and we list the details below.

Other options include an out-and-back crossing – not as far-fetched as it sounds, as the amount of re-ascent isn't terrible; or a truncated circular route, which is also detailed in the description.

But the real Nantlle Ridge is linear, starting at the foot of Snowdon and clambering breathlessly onto its spine via the outlying summit of Y Garn (yes, another one). It then drops and climbs over a succession of tops – some, like Mynydd Drws-y-coed and Craig Cwm Silyn, memorable for some wonderful, easy scrambling; while others like Trum y Ddysgl and Mynydd Tal-y-mignedd, more so for their magnificent views.

THE NANTLLE RIDGE

DISTANCE: 10.5KM/6MILES » **TOTAL ASCENT:** 920M/3,018FT » **START GR:** SH 571525 » **FINISH GR:** SH 495510 **TIME:** 5-6 HOURS » **MAP:** OS EXPLORER OL17 SNOWDON » **REFRESHMENTS:** CWELLYN ARMS, RHYD DDU; TEA ROOMS, RHYD DDU » **TRANSPORT:** HUW'S TAXIS – T: 01286 676 767 OR 07967 881 903 – THEY WILL DROP YOU AT THE START OR COLLECT YOU FROM THE FINISH FOR JUST £5. BUSES TO RHYD-DDU FROM CAERNARFON AND BEDDGELERT » **NAVIGATION:** MAINLY CLEAR PATHS WITH SOME SHORT SECTIONS OF SCRAMBLING. THE SECTION FROM CRAIG CWM SILYN DOWN TO THE FINISH COULD BE AWKWARD TO FOLLOW IN POOR VISIBILITY.

LAMBS IN CWM PENNANT

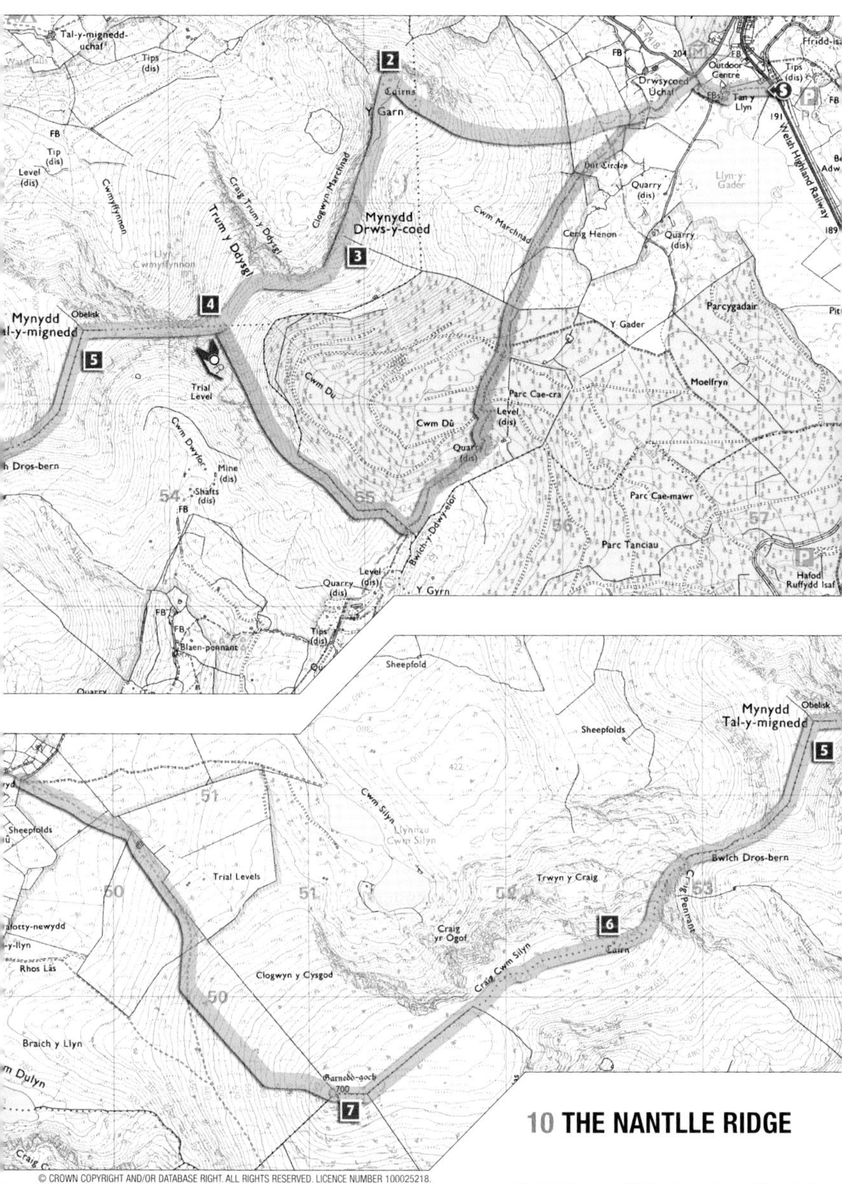

10 THE NANTLLE RIDGE

Directions – The Nantlle Ridge

S Cross the road and go through the gate opposite to follow a flagstone path to a stream, where you **turn left** to a footbridge. Cross the bridge and continue to join a good track that leads up towards a road. **Turn left**, over a stile, just before you reach the road, and follow the grassy track to a gate that leads out onto open ground. Now follow the obvious path steeply upwards until you reach a patch of scree that is best passed on the left. Cross a ladder stile and continue for a few more paces to Y Garn's summit cairn.

2 **Head left** (south) from here and follow the wall directly down into the dip. Now **keep ahead** to scramble up towards the summit of Mynydd Drws-y-coed, staying as close to the narrow and exposed crest as possible. Most of the more difficult sections can be flanked to the left. The scrambling eventually eases and a stile leads on to a rather uneventful grassy summit.

3 Drop from here and then climb again, still close to the escarpment edge, to the table-top summit of Trum y Ddysgl – a fine spot to take stock before moving on to the far end of the plateau.

OR **Optional Route – Circular Route**

As the ground starts to drop steeply, **bear left** and follow a clear path down a subsidiary ridge (heading **SSW**) with the wood to your left. This leads down into deep saddle, where a gate gives access to the wood. Take this and follow it down to a broad forest track. **Turn right**, then **immediately left**, and then continue **straight down** until you see a small stream on your left. Continue to a bridge over this and then keep **straight ahead** to follow an old wall down to the bottom edge of the forest. Keep ahead now, to follow a clear path around the foot of Mynydd Drws-y-coed and on to the flanks of Y Garn. Here you'll meet your outward route, where you **turn right** to retrace your earlier tracks back to Rhyd-Ddu.

4 To continue with the main linear route, drop into the next col, which is narrow enough to offer excellent views over both Cwmyffynnon to the north and Cwm Dyfor on the other side, and then begin the long pull up to the huge obelisk on the summit of the wonderfully-named Mynydd Tal-y-Mignedd – the Mountain at the End of the Bog.

5 Drop south from the obelisk into Bwlch Dros-bern (very steep in places), which is dissected by fence posts at the eastern end and then a wall. This leads to the foot of the next scramble, which starts on the left, but then switches right, and then switches back left again. It's only around Grade 1, and most of the awkward sections can be avoided, so choose whatever line you like, or even keep further to the right to pretty much avoid the scrambling altogether. Whatever line you choose, they all come together at the top, where a good path winds its way up to the summit cairn on Craig Cwm Silyn.

6 Keep **straight ahead**, passing close to the western cairn, and then drop slightly before climbing easily to the rock-crowned top of Garnedd-coch. The first rocky knoll is a false summit so stick to the wall until you see another wall, which you cross by a stile. The trig point, which is crumbling away, is immediately behind the wall.

7 **Turn right** here and follow the wall down, with great views over the ocean to Anglesey. At the bottom, keep ahead, over boggy ground, and you'll eventually climb over a small but still boggy hillock to meet a good track. **Turn left** onto this and follow it to the car park and the gate that leads onto the road head.

THE NANTLLE RIDGE FROM CWM PENNANT

WATERFALLS IN CWM YSTUMIAU

11 Moel Siabod

19km/12miles

A devious, lonely approach to one of Snowdonia's shapeliest peaks

Dolwyddelan » Cwm Ystumiau » Llyn y Foel » Daear Ddu » Carnedd Moel Siabod (872m) » Bwlch Rhiw'r Ychen » Carnedd Cribau » Bwlch y Rhediad » Blaenau Dolwyddelan » Dolwyddelan Castle » Dolwyddelan

Start

Street parking in the centre of Dolwyddelan or the station car park. This is on the A470 between Blaenau Ffestiniog and Betws-y-Coed. GR: SH 734524.

The Walk

What Moel Siabod, or just plain 'Siabod' as it's often referred to, lacks in height, it more than makes up for in majesty; especially when viewed from Capel Curig, where it is surely one of Snowdonia's most shapely peaks.

Capel Curig also supplies the starting point for most trade routes up the mountain, but their popularity, and the resulting well-worn paths, seem somewhat out of character with the rest of the Moelwynion range, of which Siabod reigns supreme. So an approach from the south seems somewhat more fitting.

The walk gets off to an ominous start, but the rough pasture soon gives way to easy woodland walking and this in turn leads into a wonderful, secluded cwm.

Steep walking leads to the lovely Llyn y Foel, and from here the airy ridge of Daear Ddu offers easy scrambling almost all the way to the summit. This far, the action has been centred on the better defined face of the Moelwynion, but as height is lost, so the wilder, more remote side of this great massif is revealed and the path that leads south along the ridge is a shining example of everything that's great about walking here.

It's hard to believe that at Clogwyn Bwlch-y-maen you're just a few kilometres from the Pen-y-Gwryd Hotel and the chaos associated with Snowdon. Another climb gains the wonderfully wild Garnedd y Cribau – this really does feel like the heart of the range – and then it's down to Bwlch y Rhediad to begin your descent.

This is surprisingly easy, following soft ground and good tracks. But it's not quite all over yet; there's still a visit to the impressive castle for those that enjoy their history.

MOEL SIABOD

DISTANCE: 19KM/12MILES » **TOTAL ASCENT:** 990M/3,248FT » **START GR:** SH 734524 » **TIME:** 7–8 HOURS **MAP:** OS EXPLORER OL17 SNOWDON & OL18 HARLECH, PORTHMADOG & BALA » **REFRESHMENTS:** Y GWYDYR INN, DOLWYDDELAN » **TRANSPORT:** BUSES AND TRAINS BETWEEN LLANDUDNO AND BLAENAU FFESTINIOG STOP AT DOLWYDDELAN » **NAVIGATION:** A CHALLENGING ROUTE WITH SOME UNTRACKED SECTIONS. CARE IS NEEDED TO LOCATE THE RIGHT PATH UP TO LLYN Y FOEL, AND AGAIN TO MAKE SURE THE RIGHT TRAIL IS FOLLOWED DOWN FROM THE SUMMIT. ALTHOUGH THERE'S ONLY FAINT PATHS FOR THE LATTER PART, THERE AREN'T TOO MANY OTHER OPTIONS TO CONFUSE THINGS.

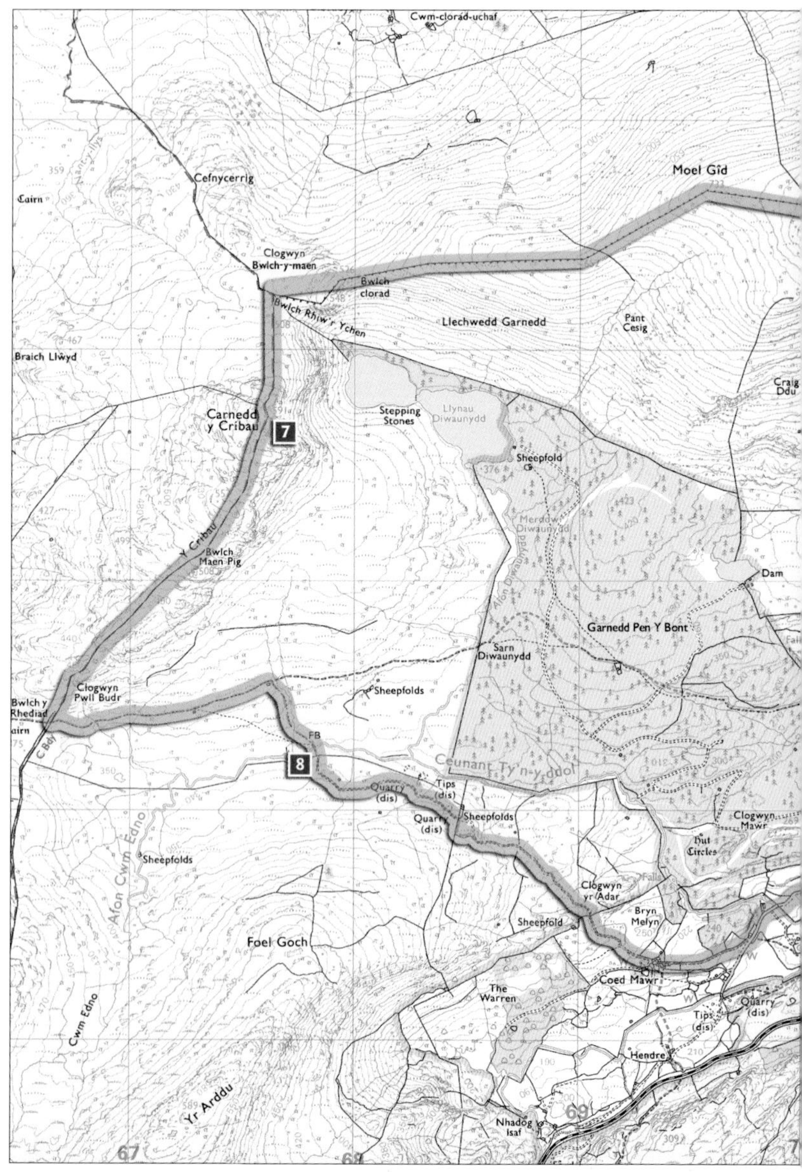

Cwm-clorad-uchaf
Moel Gîd
Cefnycerrig
Cairn
Clogwyn
Bwlch-y-maen
Bwlch
clorad
Bwlch Rhiw'r Ychen
Llechwedd Garnedd
Pant
Cesig
Braich Llwyd
Craig
Ddu
Carnedd
y Cribau
7
Stepping
Stones
Llynau
Diwaunydd
Sheepfold
Merddwr
Diwaunydd
Y Cribau
Bwlch
Maen Pig
Afon Diwaunydd
Dam
Garnedd Pen Y Bont
Sarn
Diwaunydd
Clogwyn
Pwll Budr
Sheepfolds
Bwlch y
Rhediad
FB
8
Ceunant Ty'n-y-ddol
Quarry
(dis)
Tips
(dis)
Quarry
(dis)
Sheepfolds
Clogwyn
Mawr
Hut
Circles
Afon Cwm Edno
Sheepfolds
Clogwyn
yr Adar
Bryn
Melyn
Sheepfold
Foel Goch
Coed Mawr
The
Warren
Quarry
(dis)
Tips
(dis)
Cwm Edno
Hendre
Yr Arddu
Nhadog
Isaf
67
68
69

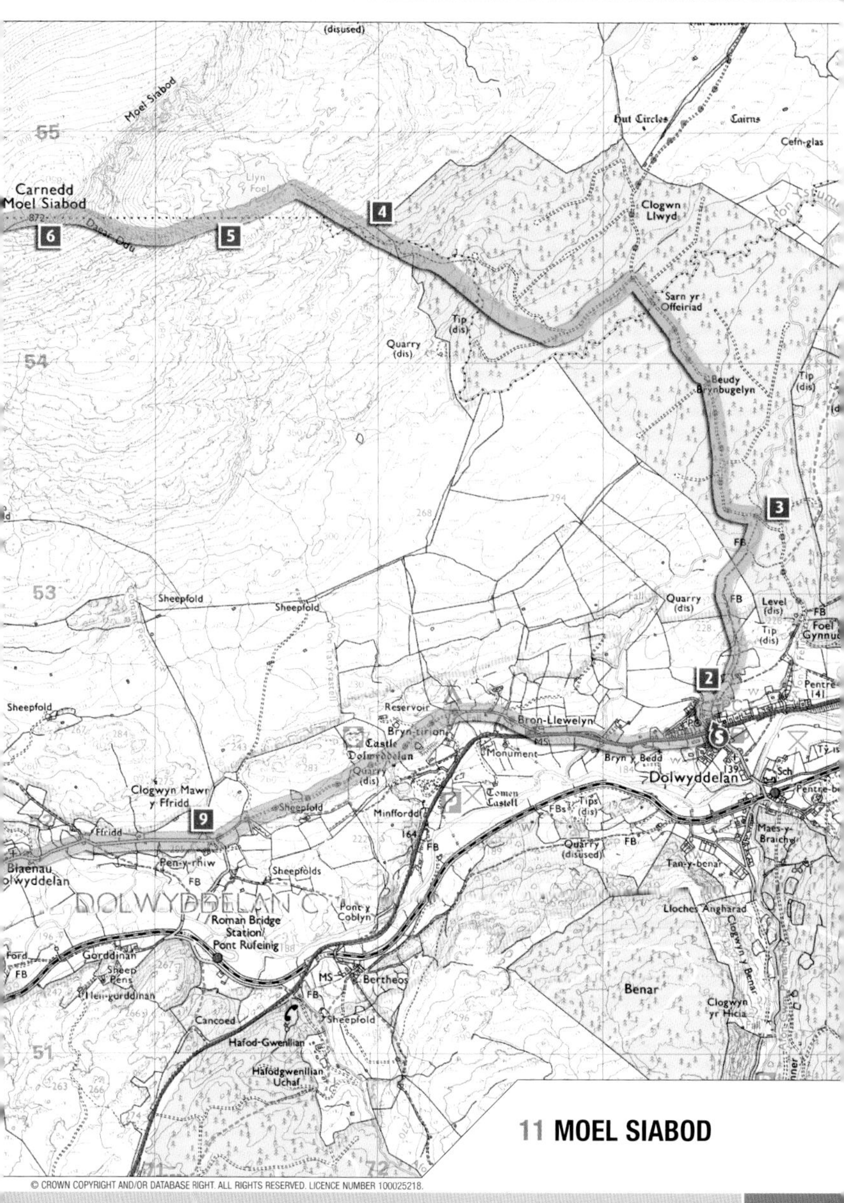

11 MOEL SIABOD

Directions – Moel Siabod

S From the main crossroads in the village, keep the Y Gwydyr Inn to your right, and the toilets to your left, and walk up the hill. Continue around to the **right**, onto a track, and then **bear left** through a kissing gate onto a footpath. Walk diagonally across the field to another gate and go through this before turning **left** to follow a very boggy path through rough ground with a house to the right.

2 Keep **straight ahead**, following occasional waymarks, and you'll eventually swing **left** over a stile. Turn **immediately right** and follow the field edge into a corner and then continue up to a step stile. Cross this and continue along the line of a tumbledown wall to another stile that leads into the forest. Cross the bridge and follow the path up to join a main forest track where you **turn left**.

3 Follow this track past a few junctions until a waymark directs you **left** onto another major forest track. Follow this around to the **right** to its end, where you cross a bridge and continue on a narrow and rough path that leads into the woods. Follow this up past a waterfall and out onto open ground.

4 Now keep the stream to your left to walk directly uphill, and where the path leaves the stream, below more waterfalls, keep **straight ahead** to climb steeply to the rocky shores of Llyn y Foel. **Turn left** to follow the moraine bank towards the foot of the obvious rocky ridge of Daear Ddu.

5 Once at the foot of the ridge, keep **straight ahead** to walk up on to it, keeping to the left of the initial steep ground and then **bearing right** to join the crest. Now enjoy easy scrambling until it eventually runs out in a deep notch close to the summit. Continue upwards on a rocky path but keep an eye open for a chance to head back right again as there's another short scramble to be enjoyed before you finally reach the trig point.

6 From the summit, head **west** to a stile over a fence and continue over a rocky knoll and down into Bwlch Rhiw'r Ychen. Now follow the fence to another stile, and cross this to climb steeply onto Carnedd y Cribau, which is crowned with a small pool.

7 **Keep ahead** to drop into the next saddle of Bwlch y Rhediad, where a stile on the **left** gives access to a boggy path that leads down into the expanses of Cwm Edno. Follow this across the hillside and pass a ruined building on the right before **turning right** onto a faint and boggy path that drops down to a flagstone bridge over a stream.

8 Cross this and climb to a stile that leads onto a broad track. **Turn left** onto this and follow it for some distance, rounding the foot of Yr Arddu and continuing through a couple of gates to pass through Coed Mawr Farm. Continue to a junction with a small lane and **turn left** onto this to follow it past houses and on up to the farm at Pen y Rhiw.

9 Here, turn left onto a waymarked track and follow this up, keeping **right** at a fork at the top. Now continue over the hill and down past the remains of Dolwyddelan Castle and keep ahead the whole time to eventually join the main road. **Turn left** to walk easily back into the village.

MOEL SIABOD FROM CAPEL CURIG

CNICHT FROM CWM CROESOR

12 Cnicht

15km/9miles

An enthralling walk up a shapely peak of modest proportions

Croesor » Cnicht (689m) » Bwlch y Rhosydd » Llyn Croesor » Moelwyn Mawr (770m) » Moelwyn Bach (710m) » Croesor

Start

Large car park at Cwm Croesor, which is signed off the A4085 at Garreg, just north of Penrhyndeudraeth. GR: SH 632447.

The Walk

From the small hamlet of Croesor, Cnicht is one of the shapeliest peaks in Snowdonia. And despite its relatively modest altitude – just 689m at its summit – it looks pretty daunting on the approach.

But any claims of being a 'Welsh Matterhorn' flatter to deceive really, and the slender summit is actually just the high point on an equally slender ridge that actually looks more 'whaleback' than pyramidal when viewed from any other perspective.

This does little to detract from the quality of this walk though, which really is one of the finest in this book. In just 15km it manages to blend everything from easy scrambling – just perfect for those that don't feel ready for the more committed lines further north – to airy walking and delicate navigation over trackless and often boggy ground.

It visits some of the area's most impressive mine ruins at Bwlch Rhosydd and Croesor – both well worth exploration – and then clambers up onto the imposing Moelwyn Mawr, an impressive peak that simply oozes grandeur despite falling well short of the 800m contour line.

The grassy plateau on top comes as something of an anti-climax after the steep push up to it, but the action hots up again soon after with a scrambly satellite peak – Craigysgafn – splitting the ridge before another steep climb leads up to the summit of Moelwyn Bach.

The descent back into Cwm Croesor is an absolute delight with soft ground beneath the feet and fine views in all directions. Even the final section on the road offers great views back up to the peaks you've just walked as well as across to the bulk of Moel Hebog just a short distance further west.

CNICHT

DISTANCE: 15KM/9MILES » **TOTAL ASCENT:** 1,150M/3,772FT » **START GR:** SH 632447 » **TIME:** 6–7 HOURS **MAP:** OS EXPLORER OL17 SNOWDON & OL18 HARLECH, PORTHMADOG & BALA » **REFRESHMENTS:** CAFÉ NEAR THE CAR PARK » **TRANSPORT:** BUSES FROM PORTHMADOG TO CROESOR » **NAVIGATION:** SOME CLEAR PATHS, BUT SOME VERY AWKWARD SECTIONS, ESPECIALLY BETWEEN CNICHT AND BWLCH RHOSYDD. IF THE VISIBILITY IS POOR, IT'S PROBABLY PRUDENT TO TURN AROUND ON CNICHT AND RETRACE YOUR STEPS BACK.

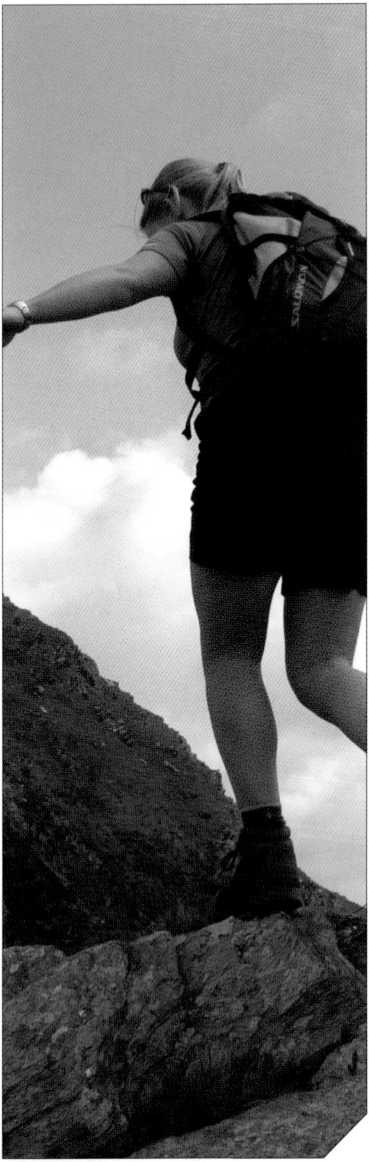

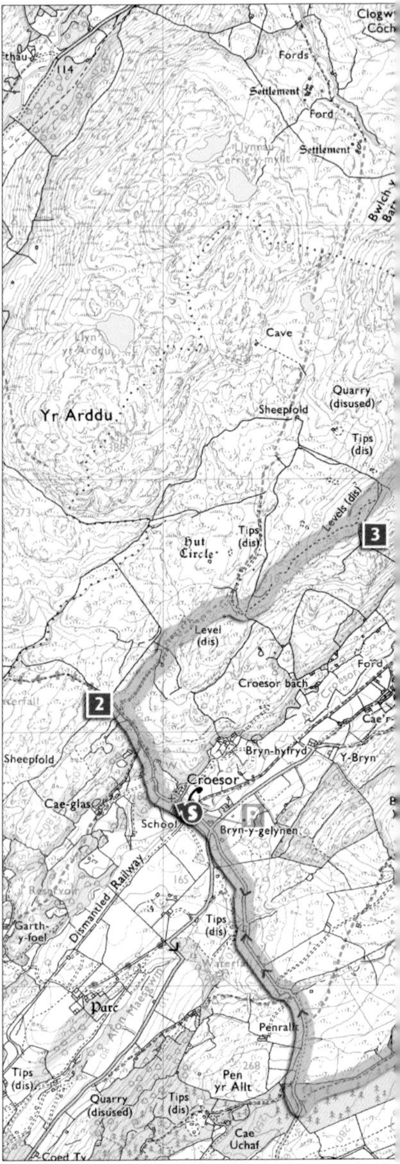

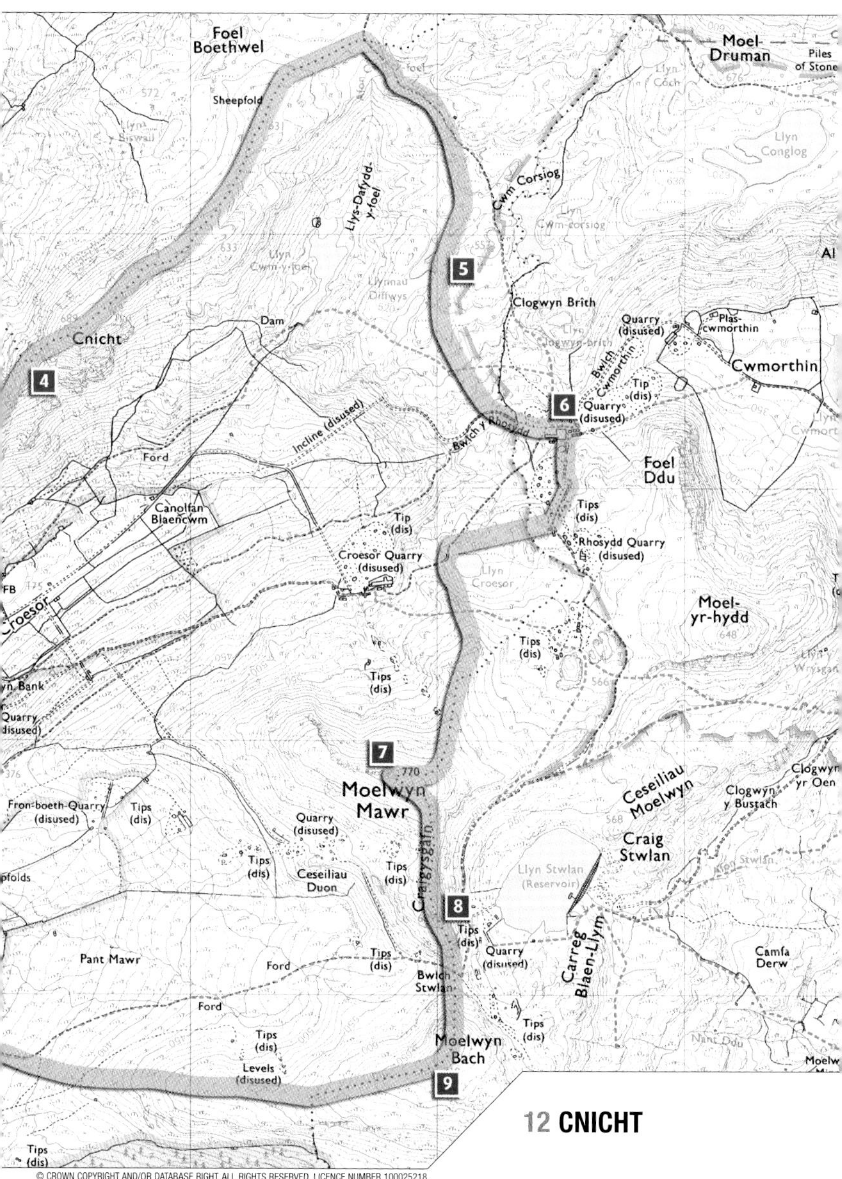
Foel
Boethwel
Sheepfold
Moel-
Druman
Piles
of Stone
Llyn
Conglog
Cwm Corsiog
Llys-Dafydd-
y-foel
Llyn
Cwm-y-foel
Llynnau
Diffwys
Clogwyn Brith
Cnicht
Dam
Quarry
(disused)
Plas-
cwmorthin
Cwmorthin
Bwlch
Cwmorthin
Tip
(dis)
Quarry
(disused)
Incline (disused)
Bwlch y Rhosydd
Ford
Foel
Ddu
Canolfan
Blaencwm
Tip
(dis)
Tips
(dis)
Rhosydd Quarry
(disused)
Croesor Quarry
(disused)
Llyn
Croesor
Croesor
Moel-
yr-hydd
Tips
(dis)
Tips
(dis)
Quarry
(disused)
770
Moelwyn
Mawr
Ceseiliau
Moelwyn
Clogwyn
yr Oen
Clogwyn
y Bustach
Fron-boeth Quarry
(disused)
Tips
(dis)
Quarry
(disused)
Craig
Stwlan
Tips
(dis)
Ceseiliau
Duon
Tips
(dis)
Craigysgafn
Llyn Stwlan
(Reservoir)
Tips
(dis)
Quarry
(disused)
Carreg
Blaen-Llym
Camfa
Derw
Pant Mawr
Ford
Tips
(dis)
Bwlch
Stwlan
Ford
Tips
(dis)
Moelwyn
Bach
Tips
(dis)
Levels
(disused)
Tips
(dis)
4
5
6
7
8
9

12 CNICHT

Directions – Cnicht

S Walk back out of the car park, past the interpretation board, and then **turn right** to walk along the road to its end. Continue **straight ahead** through the gate and along a rough track and at the top, **bear right**, again well signed, through another gate to head almost directly towards Cnicht's shapely summit.

2 Now follow the obvious rough path as it runs along the north flanks of the ridge, crossing a succession of stiles, and eventually delivering you on the crest of the ridge, where you continue upwards, mainly on a clear path. This will lead to a broad grassy notch with a steep slab ahead. For an easy scramble, **keep ahead** and slightly right to climb a stepped fault line, or if you'd prefer not to use your hands, drop further to the right to gain a good path that bypasses the difficulties.

3 Once over this section, continue upwards either on the ridge crest, which offers further scrambling opportunities, or on the path. Both will lead to the first summit, which at 689m is the true summit and offers superb views over Moelwyn Mawr as well as the rest of the walk.

4 Continue over two subsidiary summits before dropping to a fork. **Bear left** to take the best path towards Llyn yr Adar and as you reach the far end of this, **bear right** onto a rougher path that drops beneath a crag into a shallow valley. Stay with the path as it climbs again, and then **keep right** over a short, scrambly section to follow a very faint path along the eastern shores of Llynnau Diffwys.

5 Continue in the same direction and wind your way across the boggy, undulating ground, eventually dropping to join a quarry track near Bwlch y Rhosydd. **Turn left** onto this to head towards the ruined mine buildings and then **bear right** across the rubble-strewn ground to the orderly rows of buildings.

6 A fast flowing stream runs past the buildings. Follow this uphill, past a shaft, to a steep incline that follows the left-hand edge of a huge slag heap. **Bear right** over a stile at the top and follow a clear path above Llyn Croesor and on to a bridged section. As it drops again, **bear left** and climb the steep hillside to the summit of Moelwyn Mawr.

7 The ground to the south is far too steep to descend directly, so backtrack for 100m and **bear right (south)** to locate another path that now drops through rocky outcrops into the deep saddle beneath Craigysgafn. Cross this and continue **straight ahead** to scramble easily up to the summit.

8 **Keep ahead** again to drop into another saddle that lies at the foot of Moelwyn Bach and from here, it's easy to see a narrow path that heads steeply up from the saddle, gradually traversing diagonally across the hillside. Take this and cross a band of scree before continuing onto a grassy shoulder close to the summit. This is crowned with a few narrow rocks bands and a small cairn.

9 To descend, locate a faint path that leads from the cairn down onto the crest of the ridge and then follow it easily down for nearly 2km, eventually forking **right** near the bottom to aim for the right hand corner of a plantation. Continue through the gate and along the side of the wood to the road. **Turn right** to return to Croesor.

CNICT FROM THE SOUTH-WEST RIDGE

SOUTHERN MOELWYNION

DISTANCE: 12KM/8MILES » **TOTAL ASCENT:** 950M/3,116FT » **START GR:** SH 682454 » **TIME:** 6–7 HOURS **MAP:** OS EXPLORER OL17 SNOWDON & OL18 HARLECH, PORTHMADOG & BALA » **REFRESHMENTS:** CAFÉ ON ACCESS ROAD TO RAILWAY AND DAM » **TRANSPORT:** BUSES AND TRAINS TO BLAENAU FFESTINIOG REFRESHMENTS: CAFÉ BENEATH THE STWLAN DAM » **NAVIGATION:** SOME MINING TRACKS BUT MANY UNTRACKED SECTIONS WHERE NAVIGATION WOULD BE DIFFICULT IF THE VISIBILITY IS POOR.

NORTH TO SNOWDON FROM ALLT-FAWR

13 Southern Moelwynion

12km/8miles

Wild and enthralling walking from the less glamorous side of the Moelwynion

Cwmorthin » Allt Fawr (698m) » Moel Druman (676m) » Llyn Croesor » Moelwyn Mawr (770m) » Bwlch Stwlan » Cwmorthin

Start

Car park at Tanygrisiau, at the foot of Cwmorthin. This is a few miles west of the A470 at Blaenau Ffestiniog. GR: SH 682454.

The Walk

From the north, the Moelwynion mountains conceal their industrial heritage well. But approach the range from the south and there's no escaping the fact that these hills once proudly proclaimed to 'roof the world'. But the slate quarries and mines do little to detract from the quality of the walking hereabouts, in fact, it could be argued that they add something: demonstrating perhaps that man's labours sometimes appear to know no bounds.

The walk starts by tramping easily up into the expanses of Cwmorthin, passing a monument that marks a once-pristine slate garden, kept by a now deceased ex-quarry worker named Robin Jones. It then follows quarry tracks up onto the surrounding hillsides before breaking free and clambering up onto a remote ridge. The character changes radically from here with faint paths and great views north to the main Snowdonia massifs.

The rounded grassy summits that give the range their name run one into another for a while and then there's an awkward stretch that leads to the amazing mine ruins at Bwlch Rhosydd. This area was quarried in the 1830s and then mining began not long after that. The underground complex beneath your feet consists of over 170 chambers spread over 14 different floors. Mining ceased in 1930 and most of the lower chambers are now flooded. It's hard to decide whether these austere skeletons are a scar or a beauty spot really, but they are definitely worth taking a little time to explore.

Then it's the big one: Moelwyn Mawr, which at 770m is the second highest of the range and an imposing presence too. Getting off involves easy scrambling and then it's down to the ruins of the Wrysgan Mine, where a subterranean finish awaits.

MOELWYN MAWR

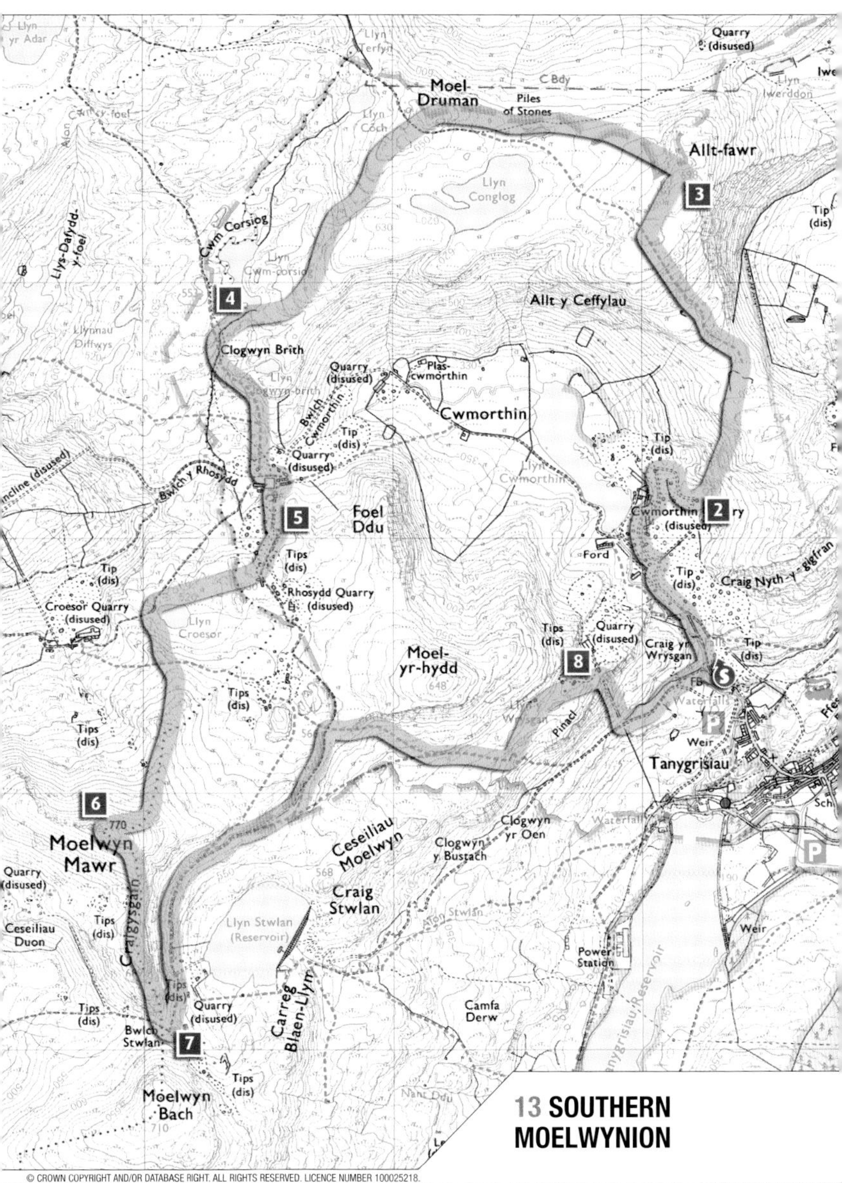

13 SOUTHERN MOELWYNION

Directions – Southern Moelwynion

S Go through the barrier and head up the main track into Cwmorthin. Pass waterfalls on your left and a monument on the other side of the stream. **Turn right** at the obvious fork, and climb up above the lake and **bear right** onto another track. Follow this around a sharp right hand bend and continue beyond the spoil, where a faint path leads uphill to the ridge above.

2 **Bear left** upon reaching the top, and follow the ridge along until you locate a clear path that climbs easily up to a cairn that marks a subsidiary top. Look half right here and you'll see the main top of Allt-Fawr, which is easily reached via a faint path.

3 **Turn left** onto the slender summit and follow the ridge down slightly, and then **bear right** (**west**) to follow the fence down past the shores of a small lake and up onto the unmarked top of Moel Druman. **Note**: the next section is quite difficult to follow so care is needed with navigation. **Bear left** (**south west**) to follow the ridge for 500m to a small lake (extension of Llyn Conglog). **Turn right** to follow the stream to the tip of Llyn Cwm Corsiog.

4 Cross the dam, once a tramway, and continue in the same direction for a few metres until you meet a path by a fence. **Turn left** and follow this down to the deserted quarry barracks at Bwlch Rhosydd.

5 To the left of a huge spoil heap is a steep incline, with a shaft at its base. Walk up this to the top, and **bear right** over a stile. Now follow the path above Llyn Croesor and on to a bridged section. As it starts to drop, **bear left** and climb the steep hillside, keeping to the right-hand edge of the ridge. Continue to the summit of Moelwyn Mawr, which at 770m is the highest point of the walk.

6 The ground to the south is steep so **backtrack** for 150m to pick up a narrow path that drops east then south into the obvious saddle above Llyn Stwlan. Continue along the escarpment edge, over Craigysgafn, and steeply down into Bwlch Stwlan.

7 **Bear left** at the cairn, and follow the path back on yourself. Keep high at a fork above mine ruins, and follow the track around the hillside, far above Llyn Stwlan. Continue to a gate in the saddle between Moelwyn Mawr and Moel-y-hydd. **Bear right (don't** go through the gate) and drop slightly on a clear path that soon levels to traverse the hillside. Continue past a small lake – Llyn y Wrysgan – and then drop down an old incline, with open shafts to your left.

8 **Turn right** when you reach the buildings at the bottom and follow the cutting to the entrance of a tunnel, which you then walk though. Continue steeply down the incline on the other side and **turn left** onto the road at the bottom. **Fork left** onto a footpath at a sharp bend, and follow this back to the car park.

SUNSET FROM BWLCH STWLAN

DIFFWYS WITH SNOWDON IN THE BACKGROUND

14 The Northern Rhinogydd

13km/8miles

A short but demanding hike around the rarely visited peaks at the northern end of the range

Llyn Tecwyn Isaf » Bryn Cader Faner » Llyn Dywarchen » Moel Ysgyfarnogod (623m) » Foel Penolau (614m) » Moel y Gyrafolen (535m) » Cwm Moch » Llyn Tecwyn Isaf

Start

Small car park next to Llyn Tecwyn Isaf, which is reached by following minor roads east from the A496, just north of Talsarnau. GR: SH 629371.

The Walk

The Rhinogydd massif has a reputation for difficult walking on rough ground, and nowhere is this more appropriate than at the very northern end of the range, where there are few paths and even fewer fellow walkers. But this shouldn't deter the pioneer; these are some of the most interesting hills in the whole of the national park and all you need is a good, clear day and some careful map reading and you're guaranteed a truly memorable outing.

The walk starts at the lovely Llyn Tecwyn Isaf, to the west of the range, and it then follows clear tracks most of the way up onto the main ridge, resorting to a bit of straightforward freelancing only at the very top. Along the way, it passes the atmospheric cairn circle of Bryn Cader Faner, one of the most impressive in Wales.

The first peak, Moel Ysgyfarnogod, is the tallest of the day, and a wonderful viewpoint with fine vistas in all directions. But it also marks the end of the more straightforward going and as you wander northwards towards Foel Penlau, the grassy hillsides are swallowed up by gritstone outcrops. The peak itself is a turreted castle that needs a devious approach to avoid a real rock climbing experience.

Diffwys is less forbidding but still consists of a fascinating blend of rock and bog that will make for difficult going if care isn't taken on route choice. Moel y Gyrafolen provides the final summit then there's more trackless going to drop into the remote Cwm Moch. From here, good paths lead to the finish.

For the non-Welsh-speakers, Moel Ysgyfarnogod means 'Rounded or Bare Hill of the Hare' and is pronounced 'Moyle (think Radio 1 DJ in singular) Usg-uh-varn-uh-god).

THE NORTHERN RHINOGYDD

DISTANCE: 13KM/8MILES » **TOTAL ASCENT:** 780M/2,559FT » **START GR:** SH 629371 » **TIME:** 6-7 HOURS **MAP:** OS EXPLORER OL18 HARLECH, PORTHMADOG & BALA » **REFRESHMENTS:** NONE » **TRANSPORT:** BUSES AS FAR AS CILFOR OR TRAIN TO LLANDECWYN STATION » **NAVIGATION:** MAINLY FAINT OR NON-EXISTENT PATHS WITH SOME EASY SCRAMBLING REQUIRED IN PLACES. BEST SAVED FOR A GOOD DAY.

MOEL YSGYFARNOGOD

14 THE NORTHERN RHINOGYDD

Directions – The Northern Rhinogydd

1 Keep the lake to your right and continue along the road, ignoring a left fork. Take the first turning on the **right** after 400m and follow this up to a gate on the left that leads to Caerwych Farm. Walk up the zigzag drive and through the farmyard. Pass through a gate at the end of the buildings and then **turn immediately right** onto a grassy track. Follow this up through sheep pastures and **keep left** at a fork to go through a gate beneath an obvious outcrop (Y Gyrn).

2 Continue on the clear path and follow well-spaced posts around the head of a bog to a clear junction with another footpath. Keep **straight ahead** and then **bear left** to climb to the amazing cairn circle of Bryn Cader Faner, visible on the skyline.

3 Here, **turn right** to follow a faint path down to and then across the brook issuing from the lake. Now strike up the grassy hillside, heading **south-east** so as to aim-off slightly, until you reach a clear track that runs east-west from the shores of the kidney shaped Llyn Dywarchen. The easiest line follows the left side of an obvious gulley that rises from the southern tip of the lower lake.

4 Once at Llyn Dywarchen, **bear right** to keep it to your left, and follow raised ground **south-east** to climb to a clear col west of Moel Ysgyfarnogod. Bear slightly **left** in the col and follow faint tracks **north east** up onto the shoulder of the mountain. Head **south-east** to the trig point and cairn.

5 **Keep ahead** to drop slightly; then **keep left** at a fork to drop into another col directly beneath the rocky walls of Foel Penolau. **Bear right** to go through a gap by a wall, then **bear left** to climb up onto the peak, continuing between the rocky outcrops until you can **bear left** again and scramble easily to the summit cairn.

6 Retrace your steps off the rocks and then **bear left** to continue between the outcrops to the far end, where you can **bear right** to contour around to a narrow path that drops alongside a wall. Continue over awkward ground onto Diffwys – a cocktail of small crags and soggy bogs – and then keep the steep ground to your right to locate a path that drops down a wall into another deep col.

7 Cross the ladder stile and follow a clear path up onto Moel y Gyrafolen's summit cairn. Now continue **north** to drop down the north ridge, following the route of least resistance, to cut into a clear path that will then drop you easily into the Cwm Moch.

8 Follow this down across a flagstone bridge and up to a ladder stile, and then continue to a gap in the wall on the right where a grassy path leads to a ruined building. **Bear left** through a gap in the wall and then **turn right** to follow a vague path over boggy ground where it soon becomes clear and stony and drops to the farmstead at Nant Pasgan Bâch.

9 **Turn left** here onto the drive and follow it down to Caerwych, where you retrace your outward steps all the way back to Llyn Tecwyn Isaf.

THE LOVELY LLYN TECWYN ISAF

RHINOG FAWR FROM LLYN DU

15 Rhinog Fawr from the East

9km/6miles

A short, sharp exploration of the most forbidding of the Rhinogydd peaks

Craigddu-isaf » Bwlch Drws-Ardudwy » Rhinog Fawr (720m) » Llyn Du » Craigddu-isaf

Start

Small car park at the road head on a minor road that runs west from A470, just a couple of miles north of Coed y Brenin. GR: SH 684302.

The Walk

If you needed proof that the Rhinogydd have attitude, this walk will provide it. The highest point is only 720m – less than 500m above the start – yet it can feel like a hill twice as high at times. There's basically no easy way to the top. The ridge-like summit is guarded by a succession of gritstone outcrops that tend to be vertical or steeper; and any route that flanks them needs to scale steep tongues of scree – often shrouded in a blanket of heather. But height is gained quickly, and the views from the top are wonderful, with the sea just a few miles west, and pretty much the whole of Snowdonia stretching off to the north, east and south.

The walk starts easily enough on comfortable old forest tracks that provide a civilised warm up. But once on open ground things turn a little tougher, but at least you can see where you are going by now. A rocky and often wet path then makes a beeline for the ambient Bwlch Drws-Ardudwy – a narrow cleft that separates the two main mountains. This would have once been a major pass.

The climb onto Rhinog Fawr is brutal – a vague, almost vertical path up a scree-filled gully that barely relents from bottom to top. Once up, that's it though and the cairn-peppered summit plateau offers scenic respite. The descent is almost as steep, and navigation is awkward in places. But the sheltered shores of Llyn Du mark the end of the worst of it, and also make a marvellous place to take a breather. More rough and often wet trails lead back into the forest and a gentle riverside stroll wraps it all up.

RHINOG FAWR FROM THE EAST

DISTANCE: 9KM/6MILES » **TOTAL ASCENT:** 600M/1,968FT » **START GR:** SH 684302 » **TIME:** 5 HOURS **MAP:** OS EXPLORER OL18 HARLECH, PORTHMADOG & BALA » **REFRESHMENTS:** NONE » **TRANSPORT:** BUSES ONLY AS FAR AS THE A470 » **NAVIGATION:** MAINLY CLEAR PATHS BUT SOME STEEP AND LOOSE AND OTHERS WET AT TIMES. SOME EASY SCRAMBLING REQUIRED IN PLACES. BEST SAVED FOR A GOOD DAY.

Directions – Rhinog Fawr

S Carry on out of the top of the car park and **keep left** at the fork. Continue until the track bends left and keep **straight ahead** to follow a rough and boggy path through a felled area towards a farm. At the end, **turn left** onto a broad track, and ignore another track to your right signed *Roman Steps* (your descent route).

2 Fork **right** by a ruined building and continue into the forest, staying with the main track, and ignoring a left turn, until it bends left, over a bridge, where you need to **keep ahead** (signed with an arrow). Continue to a gate on the edge of open ground (*Rhinog National Nature Reserve* sign) and **keep ahead** to follow a rough track up into Bwlch Drws Ardudwy, the top of which is marked with a cairn.

3 Continue down the other side until it opens out into a large, flat amphitheatre. Here, **turn right** to follow a faint and boggy path around the edge of the flat ground, aiming for the foot of the huge apron of scree that hangs from the right flank.

4 The path then winds relentlessly up the scree, first on the right and then on the left, before continuing, just as steeply, through heather and eventually levelling slightly, with a large outcrop to the left. **Bear left** to follow the edge of the outcrop, where you may have to make a few easy scrambling moves, and then continue up a narrowing gully. Stay with the path as it leads you into a huge cleft and at the top of this the ground finally relents and you are left with an easy walk to the summit.

5 Take care to leave the summit on the right path (**north-west** then **west**) and then drop steeply, with views over Gloyw Lyn, for a few paces until you see a faint but rough path forking **right**. Take this and then drop steeply down a very rough gully to join a better path below. **Turn right** onto this and follow it easily to start with, then steeply, down towards Llyn Du, which is now visible below. Continue down until, around 30m above the lake, the path **bears right** to skirt around the south eastern tip, eventually leading to the shore by the outflow.

6 **Bear half right** here, to follow a path that runs roughly parallel with the outflow stream. Stay with this as it continues down through the heather, eventually vaulting a tumbledown wall and then dropping to a fork above the valley bottom. **Keep ahead** here – the left leads to the top of the Roman Steps – and drop to cross another wall, where you keep ahead to meet a good path.

7 **Turn right** onto this and follow it down to a gate that leads into the woods. Keep **straight ahead**, on a good path, crossing two bridges and then keeping **straight ahead** at a junction with a major forest track. Stay with this, with the stream to your left, and it eventually passes a waterfall before continuing over more open ground.

8 More easy walking leads to a junction with a major track, which is where you meet your outward leg. **Turn left** and then **right** in front of the farm, to retrace your earlier tracks back to the car park.

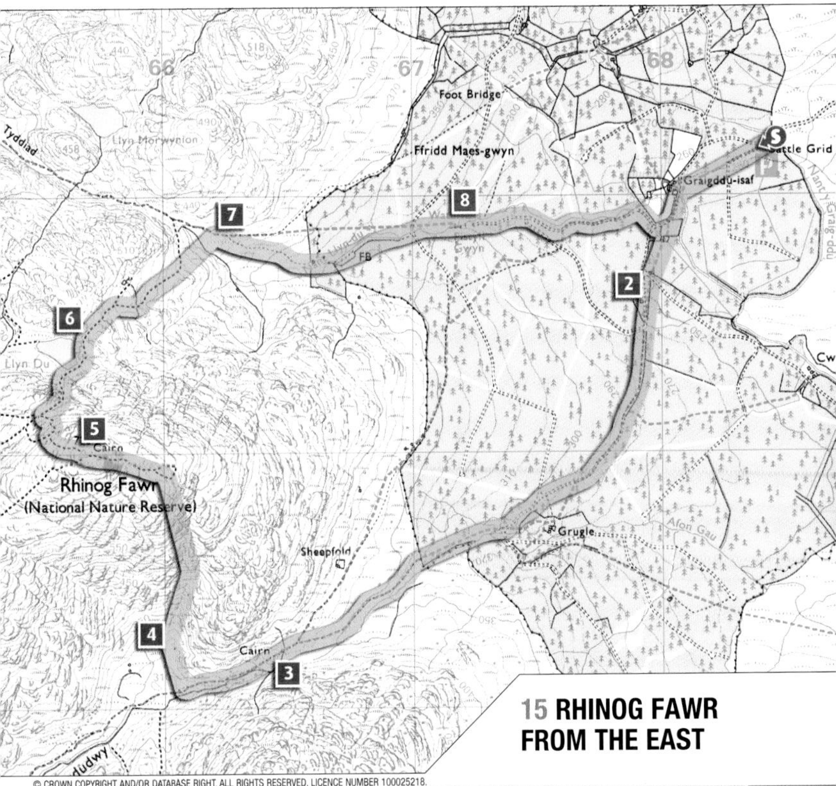

RHINOG FACH & Y LLETHR

DISTANCE: 12KM/7.5 MILES » **TOTAL ASCENT:** 830M/2,723FT » **START GR:** SH 641270 » **TIME:** 6 HOURS
MAP: OS EXPLORER OL18 HARLECH, PORTHMADOG & BALA » **REFRESHMENTS:** NONE » **TRANSPORT:** BUSES AS FAR AS LLANBEDR, CAMBRIAN COAST RAILWAY TO LLANBEDR » **NAVIGATION:** MAINLY ROUGH MOUNTAIN PATHS, NAVIGATION WOULD BE DIFFICULT IN POOR VISIBILITY.

ON THE FLANKS OF RHINOG FACH, RHINOG FAWR IN THE BACKGROUND

16 Rhinog Fach & Y Llethr

12km/7.5miles

Another rough and ready Rhinogydd walk that combines the wonderfully wild Rhinog Fach with the tallest peak in the range

Cwm Nantcol » Bwlch Drws-Ardudwy » Rhinog Fach (712m) » Llyn Hywel » Y Llethr (756m) » Cwm Nantcol

Start

Park in the farmyard of Maes-y-garnedd Farm (£2 at the time of writing). This is at the end of long, gated, narrow lanes that run east from the A496 between Barmouth and Harlech. GR: SH 641270.

The Walk

Although the Rhinogydd are renowned for their pathless rocky ridges and waist deep heather covering hidden boulders, the roof of the range – Y Llethr – is a different sort of peak altogether: rounded and grassy atop, looking for all the world like a misplaced Moelwyn. But before anyone gets too comfortable, the best way to climb to its 756m summit is via its near neighbour Rhinog Fach, and the southernmost of the Rhinog twins is every bit as rugged as its taller sibling thereby making sure that normal service is resumed.

The walks starts to the west, in the wonderfully remote Cwm Nantcol. And the work starts before you even park with an almost endless succession of gates on the tiny lanes that penetrate the valley. This is a good walk to take a passenger along. From Maes-y-garnedd, a clear, though in places wet, path leads across sheep pasture before eventually jacking up steeply and climbing into the wonderful Bwlch Drws-Ardudwy. The higher you get the more remote it feels, until you finally enter the steep-walled pass itself, where you really do feel as if someone has just closed a door behind you.

The eastern end of the pass shines a light at you though, and the route aims for this before breaking right and climbing steeply between countless outcrops and boulders to the 712m summit. This is the hard work done now and the descent is a lot more pleasant than the climb. It delivers you on the heather-clad shores of the stunning Llyn Hywel, providing an old stone wall as a handrail both down and then up again. Y Llethr relents easily from the top of the shelf.

The descent feels more like mid Wales than Snowdonia – marshy and featureless, but thankfully with a wall to guide you, and some wonderful views over the coast to keep your mind off the sore knees.

Directions – Rhinog Fach & Y Llethr

S Pay to park in the farmhouse (£2 at the time of writing) and then cross the access track to head **north-east** onto an obvious path that leads over boggy ground to a stile. Cross this and follow the clear path, with a wall to your right, all the way up to the obvious narrow pass of Bwlch Drws-Ardudwy. Continue to the top of the pass where a large cairn marks the highest point.

2 Continue beyond the cairn for a few metres and then **turn right** through a gap in the wall by a nature reserve information board. **Turn right** to go through a gap in an adjacent wall and follow a faint, narrow path directly up through the heather to the right of some scree. The first section of the climb is steep with a few awkward steps on greasy rock, but this does ease as the path tracks around the back of the hill, winding its way through numerous rock bands to an obvious fork. **Keep right** here and continue to a cairn, where you **turn left**, to continue climbing past another false summit to the true top – identified by a wall running from it.

3 Keep the wall to your left and drop down for 100m to meet another wall, which is crossed by a ladder stile. **Turn right** here to descend steeply to the shores of Llyn Hywel. The lake is surrounded by a number of rocky outcrops that offer shelter from the wind and make ideal places to pause for lunch.

4 Continue along the wall, climbing between rock bands and then up, over open ground, to the summit of Y Llethr – its bare rounded summit is somewhat disappointing in comparison to the more dramatic tops to the north.

5 The climbing is over but the descending is equally complicated so don't relax too much yet. Leave the summit by following the wall down to two step stiles at the bottom and cross the one **directly ahead** before **turning right**, now with the wall on your right. The path now tracks across a featureless landscape for nearly 2 kilometres, before bearing **half right** and dropping into the cwm below.

6 Keep **straight ahead** on a faint path that aims for the corner of a wall beneath the eastern spur of Moelfre. Follow the wall towards Moelfre where you'll pick up a faint bridleway that crosses it and drops through a succession of fields, becoming clearer as it drops. This leads onto the Cwm Nantcol road, where you **turn right** back to Maes-y-garnedd.

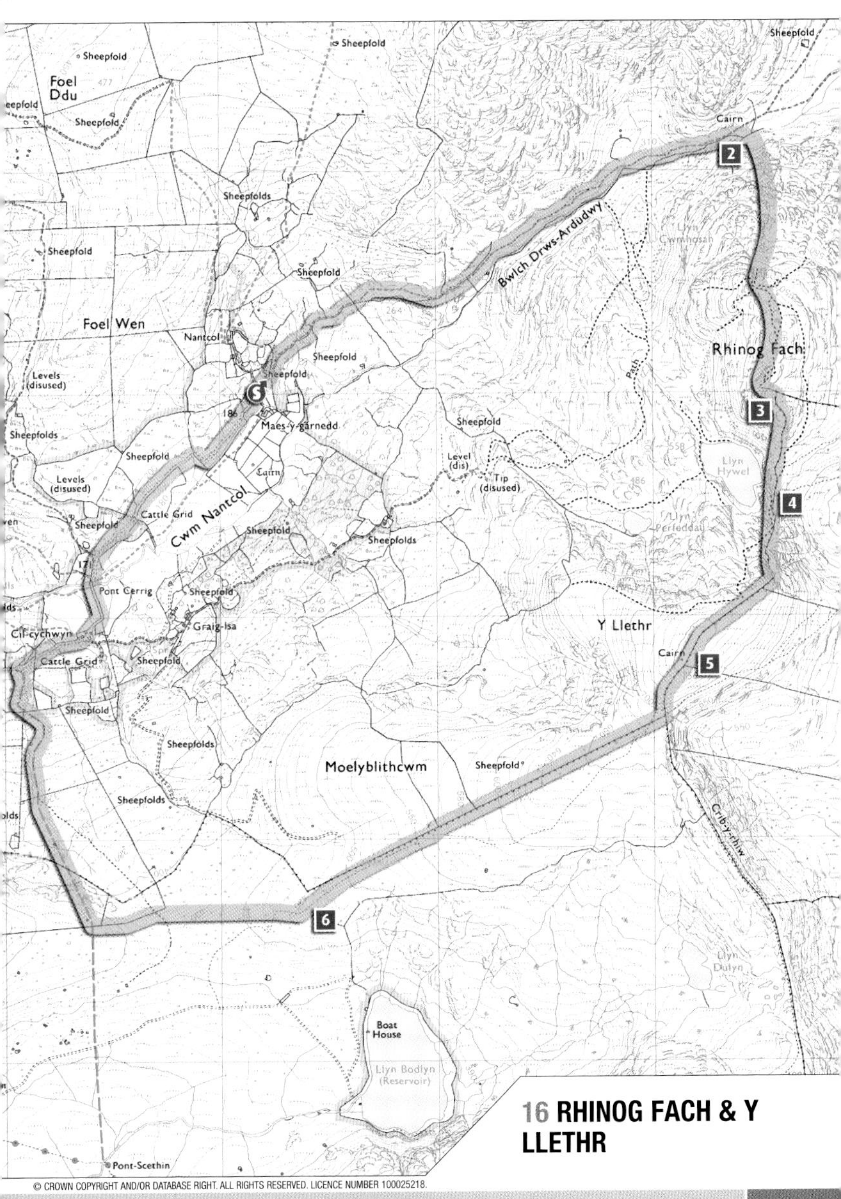

16 RHINOG FACH & Y LLETHR

SECTION 3

Southern Snowdonia

Everyone has heard of Cadair Idris. Away from Snowdon, it's Wales's most climbed peak. And it's a true gem with impressive cirques cut into both northern and southern flanks. But far fewer feet make the pilgrimage up lowly Rhobell Fawr – a peach of a mountain and a fine vantage point. And only a few more attempt the Arans, even if they do conceal the highest peak south of Snowdon. Southern Snowdonia is very different to the north, but it's every bit as enthralling as a place to walk.

CWM CYWARCH, ARANS

A FIERY SUNSET OVER CYFRWY AND CADAIR IDRIS

RHOBELL FAWR

17 Rhobell Fawr

14km/8.5miles

A rugged ramble across an impressive and seldom-visited outlier

Llanfachreth » Bwlch Goriwared » Rhobell Fawr (734m) » Ty-Newydd-y-Mynydd » Ffridd Wnion » Llanfachreth

Start

Small car park next to the school in Llanfachreth. This is on minor roads that can be reached from the A470 at Ganllwyd or the A494 between Dolgellau to Bala Road. GR: SH 755225.

The Walk

Few of Snowdonia's mountains really stand alone. Most of the peaks top lengthy ridges or wrap themselves around deeply-cloven cwms in small clusters that form obvious horseshoes. Rhobell Fawr is a definite exception, standing well over 200m above its highest col, and nearly 3km – as the raven flies – from anything that could possibly be called another summit.

It's not a high mountain: just 734m at its stone trig point; but with a lack of high ground nearby to get you started, it takes some climbing. It also makes the most of its isolated position to offer wonderful views, especially to the south west to the Cadair Idris massif and east to Aran Fawddwy and Aran Benllyn (Walk 18).

The walk starts in the hamlet of Llanfachreth, an almost magically tranquil little place, buried deep in broad-leaved woodland at the southern end of Coed y Brenin. It follows green lanes and old drove roads to the wonderful Bwlch Goriwared – a high mountain pass that would have no doubt seen a lot of traffic in days gone by.

From the pass, which is home to some beautifully restored dry stone sheepfolds, it makes a direct assault on the summit, eventually breaking free of the walls to top out among scattered outcrops. The descent is harder to follow than the climb: tracking first across confusing, rock-strewn hill-top and then dropping steeply onto a boggy plateau that gives access to much easier forest roads. These are soon left behind though, and further green lanes skirt around the southern slopes of the mountain you've just climbed. Boggy footpaths point you back west and a confusing succession of tracks, drives and footpaths then lead across sheep pasture to rejoin the outward leg above the village.

RHOBELL FAWR

DISTANCE: 14KM/8.5MILES » **TOTAL ASCENT:** 680M/2,230FT » **START GR:** SH 755225 » **TIME:** 5-6 HOURS
MAP: OS EXPLORER OL23 CADAIR IDRIS & LYN TEGID » **REFRESHMENTS:** NONE » **TRANSPORT:** NONE » **NAVIGATION:** A MIX OF GREEN LANES AND CLEAR TRACKS WITH VAGUE MOUNTAIN PATHS. THE DESCENT ROUTE COULD CAUSE PROBLEMS IN POOR VISIBILITY.

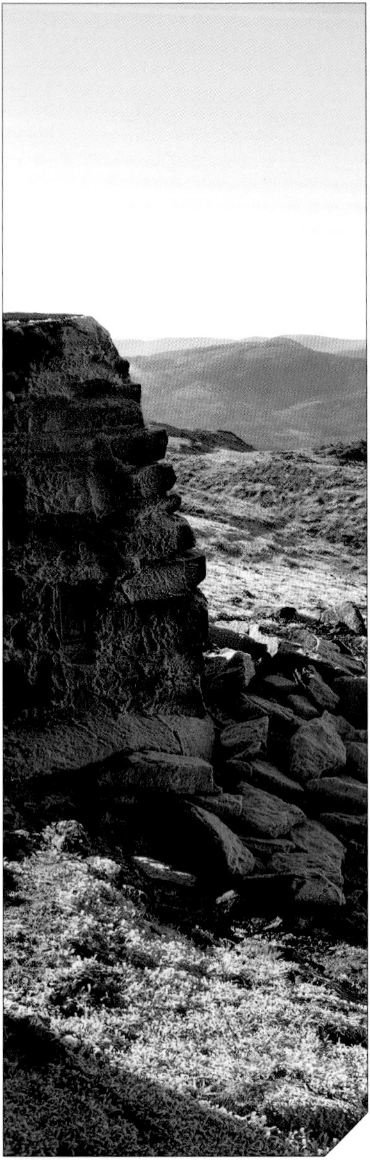

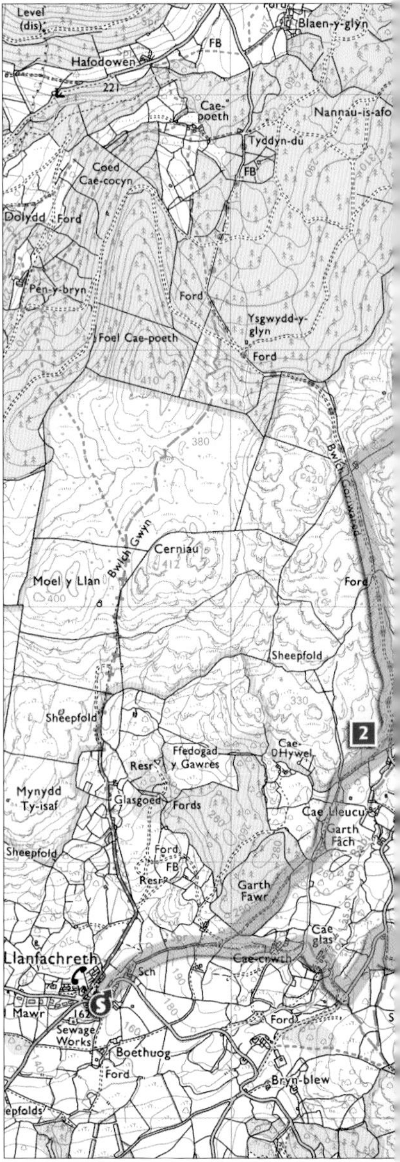
Level (dis)
Blaen-y-glyn
FB
Hafodowen
221
Cae-poeth
Tyddyn-du
Coed Cae-cocyn
FB
Dolydd
Ford
Pen-y-bryn
Ford
Ysgwydd-y-glyn
Foel Cae-poeth
Ford
410
380
420
Bwlch Gwyn
Cerniau
412
Moel y Llan
400
Ford
Sheepfold
330
Sheepfold
2
Cae-Hywel
Ffedogad y Gawres
Resr
Mynydd Ty-isaf
Glasgoed
Fords
Cae Lleucu
Garth Fâch
Sheepfold
Ford
FB
Resr
Garth Fawr
Cae glas
Llanfachreth
Cae-crwth
Sch
190
180
Mawr
162
Sewage Works
Ford
Boethuog
Ford
Bryn-blew

17 RHOBELL FAWR

Directions – Rhobell Fawr

S **Turn right** out of the car park and walk past the school and then **turn right** again to take a bridleway steeply uphill away from the village. Now follow this lovely old green lane straight upwards, eventually entering a wood. **Bear right**, through a gate and out onto sheep pasture and continue in the same direction, now with the wall to your left. Continue **straight ahead** until you eventually meet a broad track.

2 **Turn left** onto this and follow it easily up, between walls, towards Bwlch Goriwared – the obvious pass at the top. Pass the recently renovated sheepfolds on your right and then cross a ladder stile on your right to gain open ground. Now follow the wall, keeping it on your right, all the way up to Rhobell Fawr's rock-peppered summit.

3 The descent is definitely the trickiest bit of the walk. First leave the trig point to the **east**, continuing roughly on the same line as you climbed up. This will lead you to a ladder stile over a wall and beyond this, you'll find a clear but narrow path. Follow the path down and it will join another dry stone wall that will now usher you **slightly right** to another ladder stile.

4 Cross this stile and now head pretty much **straight down** the steep hillside, winding between numerous outcrops as you go. You'll eventually drop onto a broad, boggy plateau, where you keep **straight ahead** again and cross a brook beneath a steep bank. Climb the bank and keep **straight ahead** to a gate that leads onto a forest track. (**Note**: In poor visibility, it's best to follow the wall all the way down from the stile at the top although it does have a few trickier steps.)

5 **Turn right** onto the forest track and then **fork first right** at a major junction. Now contour around the hillside, always on a good track, for around 3km to a disused quarry. **Turn right** here onto a waymarked footpath and follow this steeply up to a stile at the top. Keep **straight ahead** to descend through the gorse to another stile on the right. Continue **straight ahead** through a gap in a wall to a waymark post in a dip and now follow footpath signs and stiles around to the **left** and onto a drive.

6 Walk downhill, **keeping right** to a lane and then **turn left** onto this. Now **turn right** to drop again, and follow a succession of footpath signs and stiles across sheep pasture, eventually going through a gate that leads back onto the green lane you walked up earlier. **Turn left** to retrace your earlier steps back past the school to the car park.

WILD AND REMOTE HILLSIDES ON THE APPROACH TO RHOBELL FAWR

CWM CYWARCH

18 Aran Fawddwy & Cwm Cywarch 16km/10miles

Far from the madding crowds on Southern Snowdonia's highest peak

Cwm Cywarch » Aran Fawddwy (907m) » Aran Benllyn (885m) » Aran Fawddwy (907m) » Drws Bach » Drosgl (731m) » Cwm Cywarch

Start

Car parking at Blaencywarch farm at the road head in Cwm Cywarch. This is easiest reached by following narrow lanes from Dinas Mawddwy, a few miles east of Dolgellau. GR: SH 853184.

The Walk

The Arans are so easily overlooked. They don't quite measure up to the 3,000ft mark – the highest, Aran Fawddwy, weighs in a measly 7m short of guaranteed fame and fortune. And they can't quite match the pull of the slightly lower Cadair Idris, which is just a few miles down the road but eminently easier to get to.

But this apparent snub works in the massif's favour and the walking here has a wild flavour that is so sadly missing from some of the more popular peaks. Logistics probably play a part: this is a linear landscape with few natural circuits to speak of. But this walk is the exception and what a gem it is.

It starts in Cwm Cywarch, surely one of the most beautiful valleys in this book if not in all of Wales. And it then follows a delightful tumbling brook beneath brooding cliffs to gain a lofty ridge. This is the dull section, if such a thing exists, and height is gained slowly for the next few kilometres as you hop and skip across boggy sections occasionally assisted by a boardwalk of railway sleepers.

But the summit when it comes is worth every minute. As is the neighbouring top of Aran Benllyn which is easily reached by an out-and-back sortie.

The descent is as sumptuous as the climb: first tracking around the head of the valley, with amazing views as well as a touching memorial. And then descending on a die-straight footpath that makes easy work of losing 400 vertical metres. All that's left is a gentle walk back to the car park.

For those that enjoy their stats, Aran Fawddwy isn't just the highest summit in southern Snowdonia, it's also the tallest British mountain south of Snowdon.

ARAN FAWDDWY & CWM CYWARCH

DISTANCE: 16KM/10MILES » **TOTAL ASCENT:** 900M/2,952FT » **START GR:** SH 853184 » **TIME:** 6-7 HOURS **MAP:** OS EXPLORER OL23 CADAIR IDRIS & LYN TEGID » **REFRESHMENTS:** NONE » **TRANSPORT:** LIMITED BUS SERVICES BETWEEN DOLGELLAU AND DINAS MAWDDWY. » **NAVIGATION:** MAINLY GOOD PATHS ALTHOUGH SOME BOGGY SECTIONS. SOME SECTIONS COULD BE AWKWARD IN POOR VISIBILITY.

MEMORIAL CAIRN AT DRWS BACH

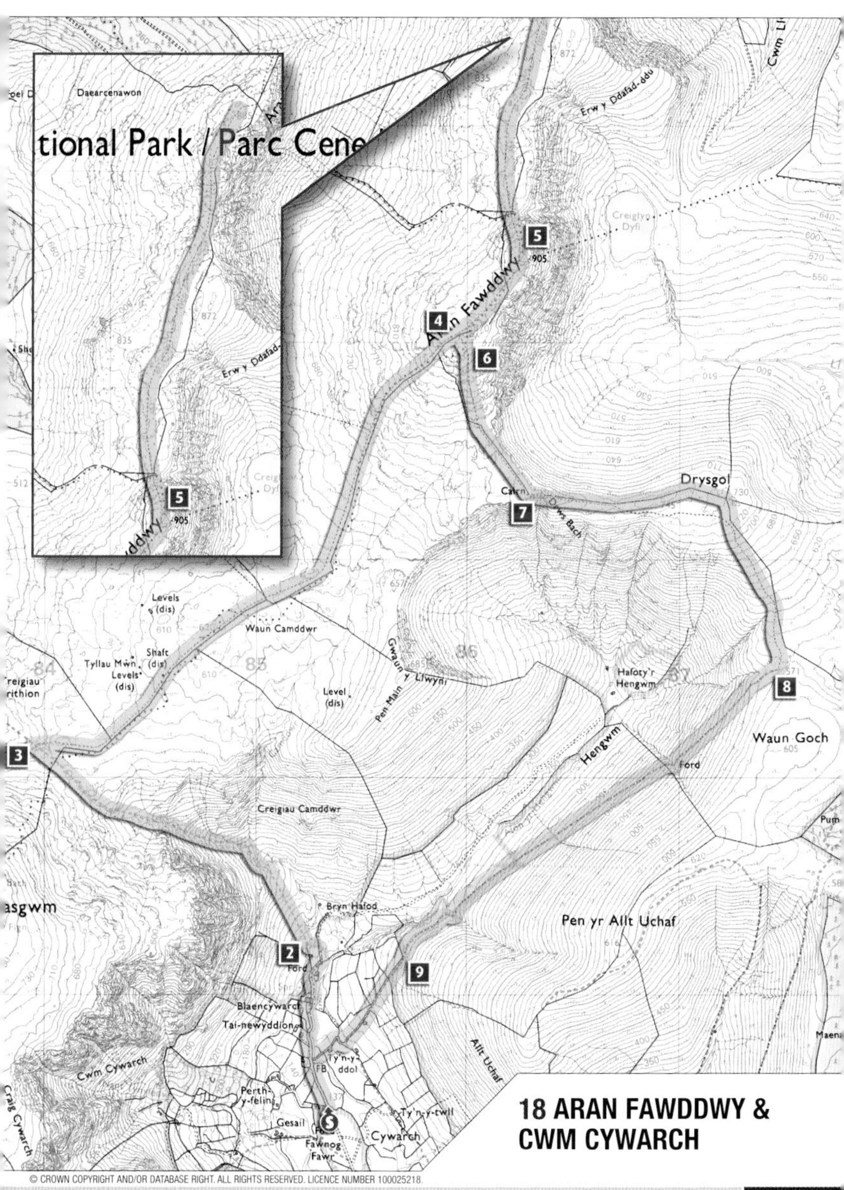

18 ARAN FAWDDWY & CWM CYWARCH

Directions – Aran Fawddwy & Cwm Cywarch

S Continue up the road to the farm of Blaencywarch and skirt around to the **right**, following clear waymarks. A gate leads onto a track which you then follow to a stile on the **left**. Cross this and follow the obvious, grassy path up and across the hillside with great views of the imposing cliffs of Craig Cywarch and Glascwm above and to the left.

2 You are aiming for the obvious notch in the skyline at the top of the ravine that carries the infant Afon Cywarch. Cross the river and continue steeply up the northern bank until the gradient eases slightly. Continue onto a broad, boggy plateau where you'll come across a small pond.

3 **Turn right** here and follow the clearly waymarked trail towards the rocky summit of Aran Fawddwy, still some 300 vertical metres above you. Continue over a succession of railway sleepers that make easy work of the boggy plateau. Eventually soft ground gives way to rock and the ground steepens and climbs to a stile at the southern end of the summit ridge.

4 **Keep ahead** to a large cairn on the southern top and continue to the trig point sitting on top of a huge pile of stones. The cliffs on the eastern side of the trig point offer shelter if needed.

5 From here, continue northwards towards Aran Benllyn. You'll cross to the left of the fence for a while before crossing back close to the summit. After bagging the peak, retrace your steps back to Aran Fawddwy and continue **south** from the trig point to the southern top.

6 Swing **slightly left** here to hug the escarpment and follow it down to a stile on a flat triangular promontory. **Keep left** on a clear path and follow it on to a short narrow arête at Drws Bach.

7 The obvious spur of Drysgol, your next objective, is now visible **straight ahead**. Pass a touching memorial to a member of the RAF Mountain Rescue Team, killed by lightning while on rescue duty close to this point, and stay on the path, which actually cuts out the summit of Drysgol by traversing to the right and dropping steeply down into the broad saddle beneath Waun Goch.

8 Here you'll pick up a footpath waymarker that directs you down to the **right**. Follow this and drop easily down on a gently sloping path that cuts a die-straight line across the steep slopes above the Afon yr Hengwm. The views of Cwm Cywarch from here are absolutely breathtaking.

9 The way ahead is easy now; continue through a couple of fields, on a well-marked path, and **keep right** as you join a sunken lane at the bottom. This leads across a footbridge and onto the road that you walked up earlier. **Turn left** to return to your car.

SOUTHERN SNOWDONIA AND THE CAMBRIAN MOUNTAINS FROM ARAN FAWDDWY

LOOKING UP TO MYNYDD MOEL FROM THE NORTH

19 Cadair Idris from the North

9km/5.5miles

A straightforward ramble over Southern Snowdonia's most popular peak

Ty-nant » Fox's Path » Llyn Gafr » Llyn y Gadair » Penygadair (893m) » Pony Path » Ty-nant

Start

There's a large pay and display car park near Ty-nant at the foot of the mountain. This is at the top of a narrow lane that leads south from Dolgellau. It is signed from the town centre. GR: SH 698152.

The Walk

Cadair Idris is at its most impressive from the north. The summit, Penygadair, sits atop vertiginous cliffs of weathered grey rock that wouldn't look out of place in the Glyderau, and the stunning Llyn y Gadair is among Wales's most beautiful mountain tarns. The views up to the peak from the road that skirts its northern flanks are guaranteed to set the pulse racing and the walking's even more enthralling.

The Fox's Path breaches the main headwall above Llyn y Gadair and leads almost directly to the summit. It's a lovely trail to start with, crossing tree-dotted sheep pasture with ease and passing the lovely Llyn Gafr before finally clambering up to the shores of Llyn y Gadair. From here, it's steep and loose and a pretty brutal way to gain the summit, but it's definitely better in ascent than descent so it's just a case of bracing yourself and pushing on.

Once up, the hard work is all over and you can enjoy the summit views, which include the nearby Arans and Rhobell Fawr as well as the taller mountains of northern Snowdonia and even Pumlumon – Mid Wales's tallest peak to the south. It's also worth diverting south for a few paces to enjoy the views over the spectacular Cwm Cau. There's plenty of shelter on this side of the summit and it's also easy to escape the crowds here.

The descent starts rough – steep and stony but at least the views compensate for the knee-pain. But it quickly eases into a good path that leads down into a deep col; and from here it zigzags sweetly back down to flat ground. The run-in back to Ty-nant is nothing more than pleasant country walking.

CADAIR IDRIS FROM THE NORTH

DISTANCE: 9KM/5.5MILES » **TOTAL ASCENT:** 760M/2,493FT » **START GR:** SH 698152 » **TIME:** 4-5 HOURS **MAP:** OS EXPLORER OL23 CADAIR IDRIS & LYN TEGID » **REFRESHMENTS:** GWERNAN LAKE HOTEL CLOSE TO THE START » **TRANSPORT:** BUSES AS FAR AS DOLGELLAU ONLY » **NAVIGATION:** MAINLY CLEAR BUT ROUGH MOUNTAIN PATHS, ONE STEEP AND LOOSE SECTION.

Directions – Cadair Idris from the North

1. **Turn left** out of the car park onto the road and continue to the Llyn Gwernan Hotel, where you **turn right**, through an iron gate, onto a clear path. This is the Fox's Path. Continue to a stile which leads onto open moorland and **stay ahead** to ford a couple of small brooks before eventually reaching another stile. **Keep ahead** here and climb steadily up to the outflow of the lovely Llyn Gafr (Lake of the goat).

2. Keep **straight ahead** for a short, sharp and very steep push up to Llyn y Gadair – a stunning mountain tarn which is guarded on three sides by daunting walls of broken rock. The jagged arête that drops from the crags on the right is the Cyfrwy Arête – a classic scramble/climb.

3. Keep the lake to your **right** and follow the path along the shores to a final push up the steep scree-covered slope. Once up follow a faint path **half right** towards the rock-crowned summit. A short walk south will also reveal the deep scoop of Cwm Cau and the towering crags of Craig Cau.

4. To descend, follow the main track, the Pony Path, **rightwards** along the escarpment edge, with great views back down over Llyn y Gadair. Stay with the main path, all the time **heading west**, and follow it easily down into the broad col that separates the main mountain from the outlying top of Carnedd Lwyd.

5. The path swings **right** here and soon becomes much steeper as it zigzags onto the huge plateau below. Stay with the path as it crosses the easier ground to a gate in a wall and then continue, as it drops steeply again, back down to the road near Ty-nant. **Turn right** onto the road and the car park is just a few metres up on the left hand side.

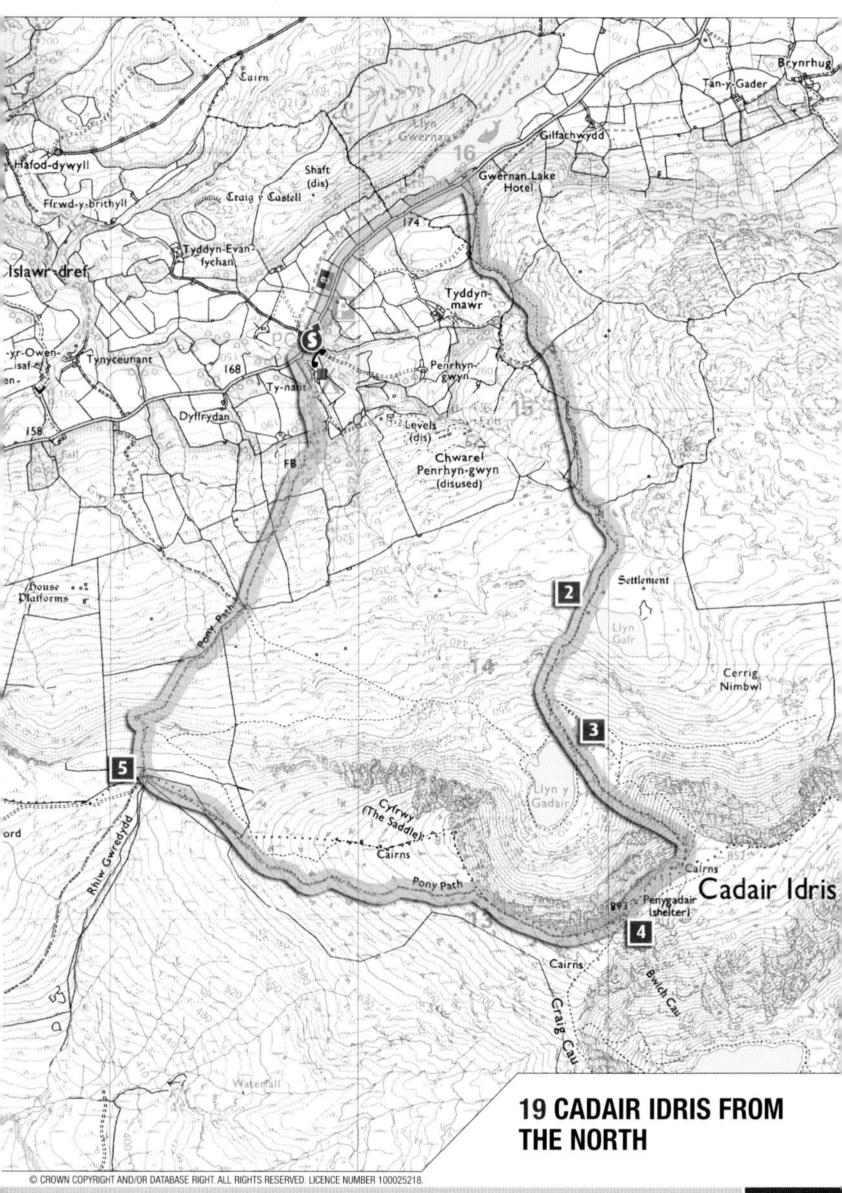

19 CADAIR IDRIS FROM THE NORTH

CRAIG CAU FROM CWM CAU

20 Cadair Idris from the Minffordd Path 9.5km/6miles

A scintillating loop around one of Snowdonia's most dramatic cwms

Dôl Idris Car Park » Minffordd Path » Llyn Cau » Craig Cau (791m) » Penygadair (893m) » Mynydd Moel (863m) » Nant Cadair » Dôl Idris Car Park

Start

The walk starts at the Dôl Idris Car Park, which is signed off the A487 at its junction with the B4405 at Tal-y-llyn – a few miles north of Corris. GR: SH 732115.

The Walk

Cwm Cau is a steep-sided, lake-filled cirque carved deeply into the southern flanks of Cadair Idris, providing southern Snowdonia's most popular peak with a southern profile that's almost as spectacular as its northern one.

It's textbook perfect – a beautiful sheltered tarn walled in by towering crags on three sides and a bank of terminal moraine on the other, with the mountain's main summit standing tall and proud above its vertiginous headwall. A lap of this stunning valley, taking in the summits of Craig Cau, Penygadair and Mynydd Moel, is about as perfect as a hill walk can be; it is without a doubt one of the finest outings in this book.

It starts with the brutally steep Minffordd Path which climbs from Dôl-y-Cae through woodland and alongside the tumbling Nant Cadair to emerge on the open slopes of Ystrad Gwyn. From here it continues ever upwards, now with great views, until it finally arrives on the shores of the stunning Llyn Cau, where the whole scene reveals itself for the first time.

From the lake it's up again – this time onto Craig Cau, and there's still more to do before the summit of Penygadair finally surrenders. The views are even better from here and on a very clear day you should be able to make out pretty much the whole of Snowdonia to the north as well as the main peaks of the Brecon Beacons, many miles to the south.

Skyline cruising leads along the ridge to Mynydd Moel – some reward for all that effort – and then it's down on a steep but clear path that rejoins the Minffordd Path at Nant Cadair.

All that's left is to retrace your steps back to the car park – thankfully this time with gravity on your side.

CADAIR IDRIS FROM THE MINFFORDD PATH

DISTANCE: 9.5KM/6MILES » **TOTAL ASCENT:** 960M/3,149FT » **START GR:** SH 732115 » **TIME:** 4–5 HOURS **MAP:** OS EXPLORER OL23 CADAIR IDRIS & LYN TEGID » **REFRESHMENTS:** NONE » **TRANSPORT:** BUSES BETWEEN MACHYNLLETH AND DOLGELLAU » **NAVIGATION:** CLEAR BUT MAINLY STEEP MOUNTAIN PATHS. THE DESCENT ROUTE COULD CAUSE PROBLEMS IN POOR VISIBILITY.

Directions – Cadair Idris from the Minffordd Path

1 Head out the top of the car park, next to the loos, and **turn right** onto the broad tree-lined lane that leads up to Dôl-y-Cae. Go through the kissing gate and **turn left** to walk beneath the house and over a bridge that spans the tumbling Nant Cadair.

2 Now **turn right** through a clearly signed gate to follow the steep, purpose-built Minffordd Path steeply up into the trees, with the raging waters of the stream to your right. The flagstone steps make reasonably easy work of the rather gruelling gradient and soon you'll emerge through a gap in a wall onto the open hillside.

3 Keep ahead for a few steps and then **bear left** when the path splits – the path to the right is your return route. Now continue around the hillside and climb easily into the mouth of Cwm Cau, where the path splits again. **Keep right** to walk past a large rocky rib to the shores of Llyn Cau.

4 Aim towards the **south-east** corner of the lake and locate a faint path that tracks back slightly before climbing steeply uphill to meet the main path in a small niche on the obvious shoulder above. A cairn marks the shoulder and the path then swings **right** to follow the narrow ridge up towards Craig Cau, with great views across the cwm to Penygadair. Stay with the ridge path and follow it around the cliff tops to a stile near the summit of Craig Cau.

5 Cross and **keep ahead** to drop into the deep saddle of Bwlch Cau, with great views over Cwm Cau and the lake. Now climb again on a clear path that winds its way over a rocky landscape to the summit. **Avoid** the temptation to straight-line this section, the boulders are interminable in places. You'll eventually **turn right** to join the main Pony Path coming up from the west.

6 Follow this to the trig point or, if you need some shelter, head just beyond where there's a small bothy – the remains of an old tea house! For a more scenic break, continue beyond the trig point to one of the many small outcrops that overlook Cwm Cau.

7 To continue, keep the bothy to your left, follow a faint path down slightly for a few paces, and then continue across a huge plateau that eventually drops into a broad, shallow saddle ahead of Mynydd Moel. Climb easily to the summit, where there's a good windbreak.

8 To descend, **bear right** to follow first the escarpment edge, and then a fence, steeply down the south ridge. Cross a stile and stay with the path, which is clear and easy to follow, and eventually you'll drop to cross the Nant Gadair on a flagstone bridge next to the path you came up on. **Turn left** here to descend all the way back to the car park.

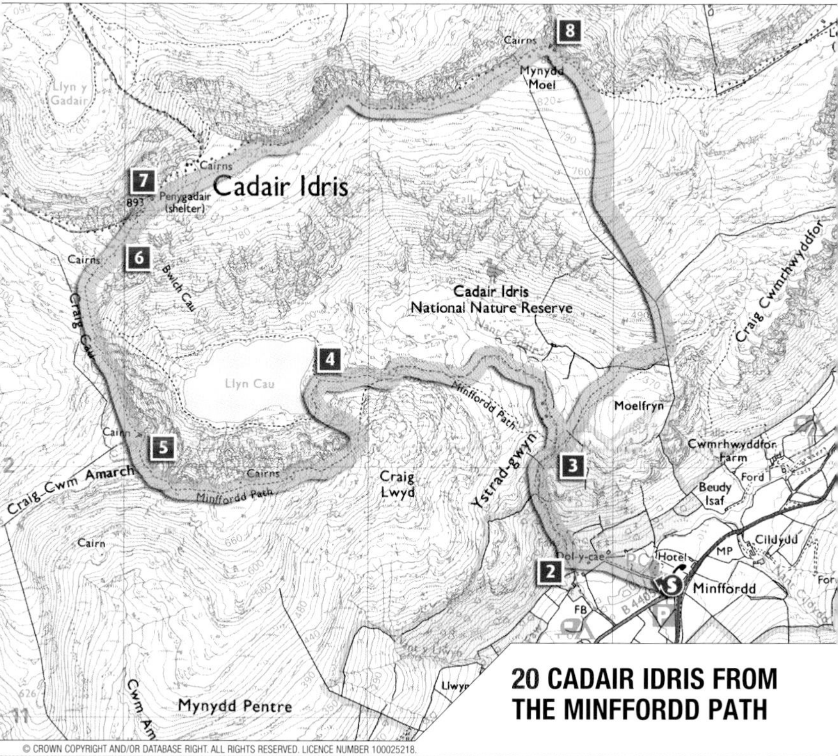

20 CADAIR IDRIS FROM THE MINFFORDD PATH

The Classic Scrambles

The Bochlwyd Horseshoe and the Snowdon Horseshoe are without doubt two of the finest mountain days you'll find anywhere. And it would seem a crime to leave them out on the basis that they require some easy scrambling. So for those that enjoy a bit of hands-on fun, or perhaps the adventurous walker that's yet to try a little of the steeper stuff, we've thrown them in for free – enjoy.

ADAM AND EVE ON THE SUMMIT OF TRYFAN

SNOWDON FROM THE CRIB GOCH PINNACLES

TRYFAN'S NORTH RIDGE

21 The Bochlwyd Horseshoe

10km/6miles

The classic Glyderau scramble – an enchainment of Tryfan's north ridge and its dramatic bristly neighbour

Llyn Ogwen » Tryfan (915m) » Glyder Fach (994m) » Bwlch y Ddwy-Glyder » Y Gribin » Llyn Ogwen

Start

Lay-by on the A5, directly beneath Tryfan's north ridge, at the eastern end of Llyn Ogwen. Easiest reached by the A5 west from Betws-y-Coed. GR: SH 663603.

The Walk

A round of the Bochlwyd Horseshoe is not so much a classic scramble but a rite of passage for scramblers everywhere. What a round it is – barely a dull moment from start to finish.

It kicks off on Tryfan's north ridge – an airy but generally friendly buttress of uber-grippy rock that appears quite muddly lower down but sharpens to a pretty impressive, almost Alpine-style, arête as it reaches the first of the summits.

There are plenty of alternative routes the whole way up, but most folk end up on the same line by the time they reach the Cannon Stone – an unlikely finger of rock that points accusingly across the Ogwen Valley towards the Carneddau. And from here on, a series of ups and downs lead to a steep final chimney that looks a lot harder than it is.

The traverse of Tryfan's summits is interrupted by an optional hop across Adam and Eve (photo p115) on the main peak – it's only a step in reality, but it's exposed enough to feel like a very big one – and then it's down into Bwlch Tryfan for more hands-on fun on Bristly Ridge.

This is a different proposition, with an awkward start and a couple of wonderfully exposed moves along the way, especially onto the pinnacles that give the ridge its name. But like Tryfan, it's all avoidable so there's no chance of starting something you can't finish.

Glyder Fach's 994m summit and a photo opportunity on the Cantilever Stone mark the top, but there's still further scrambling to be had: first on the lofty turrets of the evocative Castell-y-Gwynt (Castle of the Winds) and then on the airy spine of Y Gribin on the way back down.

THE BOCHLWYD HORSESHOE

DISTANCE: 10KM/6MILES » **TOTAL ASCENT:** 960M/3,149FT » **START GR:** SH 663603 » **TIME:** 5-6 HOURS **MAP:** OS EXPLORER OL17 SNOWDON » **REFRESHMENTS:** TEA & SNACKS IN THE IDWAL COTTAGE CAR PARK » **TRANSPORT:** BUSES SERVE THE OGWEN VALLEY FROM CAPEL CURIG » **NAVIGATION:** A GRADE 1 SCRAMBLE OVER CLEAR BUT STEEP AND EXPOSED ROCK. LOCATING THE DESCENT ROUTE FROM TRYFAN IN POOR VISIBILITY CAN BE AWKWARD.

Directions – The Bochlwyd Horseshoe

S Go through the gate beneath the obvious north ridge of Tryfan and follow the path upwards, ignoring two stiles in the wall, and then **bear left** where the wall meets the foot of the crags. Continue up along this for a couple of minutes until you reach a niche in the rock on your **right**, and start scrambling here.

2 There are many different lines on the lower stages of the route so don't worry too much about navigation, just enjoy the scrambling, aiming to stay as close to the crest as much as possible, until the ridge narrows and all paths come together. Here, keep your eyes open for a broad ledge, which boasts the Cannon Stone – a toppled flake propped against a quartz support and a great place for pictures.

3 From here, continue up the crest to another small plateau, marked with a cairn. Ahead now is a toppled flake propped against a quartz support. Pass this on the left and continue up and then down into a deep notch – best tackled to the left (facing towards the main summit). Continue upwards again to another plateau with a steep face ahead and round this to the **right** to locate a boulder-filled gulley. Scramble up this to the North Peak. Drop down from this and cross another narrow saddle to the main summit.

4 Try *Adam and Eve* – if you dare – and then continue onto the South Peak, taking care not to drop eastwards onto steeper ground. From here, you need to **break right** slightly, bypassing Far South Peak and dropping steeply on a rough path into Bwlch Tryfan.

5 Keep the wall to your **left** and climb to the foot of the first craggy outcrop. Traverse right around the base of this and then head directly up again towards a pronounced gully, which marks the start of the scrambling. Now tackle the ridge directly or flank any major obstacles on either side. The giant pinnacles offer the best sport, and are do-able at the grade if you seek out the routes of least resistance – often not obvious. But don't scramble up anything you don't think you could scramble back down. Eventually the slope relents and you'll see the summit of Glyder Fach ahead. Keep to the **left** of it to find the Cantilever Stone.

6 Now head **west**, on a reasonably clear, cairned path, and you'll soon reach the obvious pinnacles of Castell y Gwynt – the Castle of the Wind. Scramble over the top of this, enjoying some airy moves near the top, and then drop into Bwlch y Ddwy-Glyder, where two paths lead west towards Glyder Fawr.

7 Take the top path, which runs along the edge of the escarpment and hug this to a cairn that marks the top of Y Gribin ridge.

8 **Turn right** and follow the cairns down the narrowing ridge, scrambling down a few steep sections as you go – there's more scrambling over to the right, on the crest, if you fancy it. This eventually relents on a broad flat area known as the 'football pitch' where, if you keep ahead, you'll eventually reach the end of the ridge, where the path splits.

9 **Bear left** to drop steeply down into Cwm Idwal and follow the lakeside path to the A5 at Idwal Cottage. **Turn right** along the road to return to the start. (It's possible to descend to Llyn Bochlwyd and trace your way down to the road from there but the going is rough and boggy and unpleasant.)

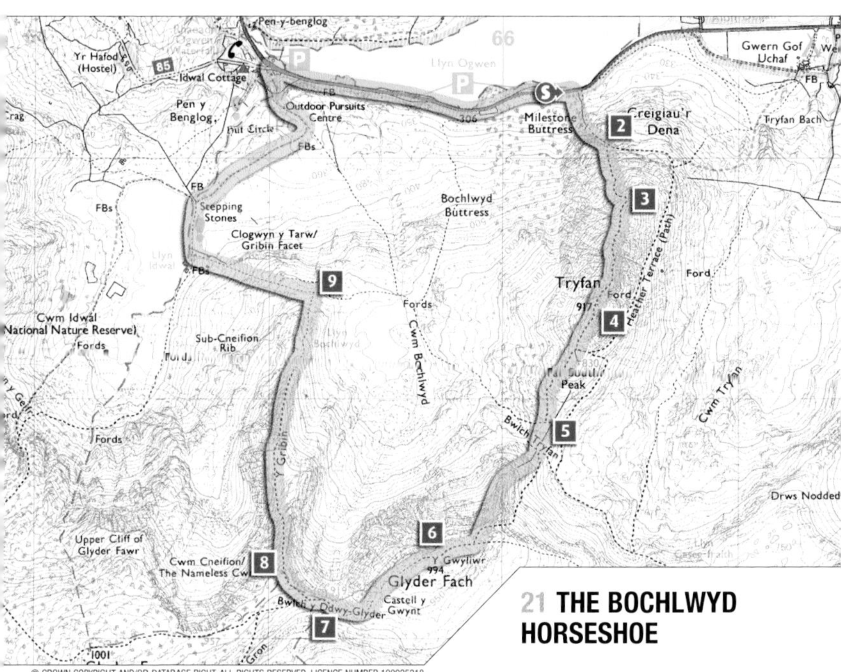

21 THE BOCHLWYD HORSESHOE

TIP-TOEING ALONG CRIB GOCH

22 The Snowdon Horseshoe

12km/7miles

Easy scrambling and breath-taking exposure on the roof of Wales

Pen-y-pass » Bwlch y Moch » Crib Goch (923m) » Garnedd Ugain (1,065m) » Snowdon (1,085m) » Bwlch y Saethau » Y Lliwedd (898m) » Pen-y-pass

Start

There's a large car park at Pen-y-pass but it fills very quickly – arrive early at busy times. GR: SH 647556.

The Walk

Few superlatives can do justice to the Snowdon Horseshoe. It is, without doubt, the best mountain walk in Wales, and it could even be a contender for the best in Britain.

So what's all the fuss about? Well firstly, it's not *all* about the scrambling. In fact it's quite a varied outing, blending the delicate, exposed traverse of Crib Goch's scary knife-edge, with plenty of straightforward, high-level, skyline walking. There's even a little easier going in places: especially towards the end with the lakeside exit along the well-surfaced yet scenic Miner's Track.

But it's Crib Goch, Garnedd Ugain and Snowdon that draw the crowds and justifiably so. Crib Goch is almost the perfect scramble: steep, scary and sufficiently exposed, yet easy enough that anybody with a head for heights could comfortably cross it. That said, a steady head is a definite prerequisite as the exposure is almost nauseating at times and this is no place to lose it.

Garnedd Ugain is a bit of a forgotten hero amongst such illustrious company, but at 1,065m it's actually the second highest summit in Wales, and its rocky spine, Crib y Ddysgl, offers plenty more scrambling for those prepared to leave the path and seek it.

The slog alongside the railway from Bwlch Glas to the summit seems almost out of character with the rest of the walk, but make an early start or come out of season and you'll enjoy it almost as much as you would have before these intrusions. You'll also enjoy a little more solitude at the top.

It would be easy to think it's all over here, but Y Lliwedd offers plenty more sport if you hug the edge, and the exposure's almost as breathtaking as Crib Goch. It's worth remembering that the face beneath your feet is home to Wales's longest rock climbs.

THE SNOWDON HORSESHOE

DISTANCE: 12KM/7MILES » **TOTAL ASCENT:** 1,170M/3,838FT » **START GR:** SH 647556 » **TIME:** 6–8 HOURS **MAP:** OS EXPLORER OL17 SNOWDON » **REFRESHMENTS:** CAFE IN THE CAR PARK AND ON THE SUMMIT » **TRANSPORT:** PEN Y PASS IS THE MAIN BUS TERMINAL SO CAN BE EASILY REACHED » **NAVIGATION:** GENERALLY EASY BUT CARE WOULD BE NEEDED IN POOR VISIBILITY – THIS IS STEEP AND DANGEROUS GROUND, AND A GOOD HEAD FOR HEIGHTS IS NEEDED ON CRIB GOCH WHICH CONTAINS SOME SECTIONS OF VERY EXPOSED BUT EASY GRADE 1 SCRAMBLING. **WARNING: THIS ROUTE BECOMES A FULL-ON MOUNTAINEERING ADVENTURE IN WINTER CONDITIONS.**

Directions – The Snowdon Horseshoe

S Head out from the top of the car park onto an obvious path, marked the Pyg Track. Follow this easily across the hillside, climbing steadily as you go until you arrive at an obvious saddle – Bwlch y Moch, where you have fine views over Llyn Llydaw and the crags of LLiwedd on the other side of the valley.

2 Leave the main path to the **right** and follow the clear path along the crest of the saddle towards the obvious blunt rock nose of Crib Goch ahead. Make as direct an assault on this as you feel comfortable with – the further right you go the easier it becomes - and after the opening steep section the gradient eases and becomes a delightful staircase of small blocky holds that lead easily up to Crib Goch's eastern summit.

3 The knife-edge section starts here. Scramble easily along it, using the crest itself for holds where the going gets steep. Continue to the first of the pinnacles, which can be scrambled easily enough or bypassed on clear paths, and you'll soon reach a second similar pinnacle. This too can be scrambled easily enough or bypassed on a narrow path. Now continue down into Bwlch Goch.

4 Ahead now lies Garnedd Ugain, which offers more scrambling for those that want it; or a good path for those that have had enough. Either way, continue along the ridge to Garnedd Ugain's 1,065m trig point and **keep ahead** to drop into Bwlch Glas, where you meet the railway line and main path up from Llanberis. Head **left** to climb steeply to the summit.

5 To descend, continue in the same direction to follow the mountain's South Ridge until you reach a tall standing stone, where you need to **turn sharp left** to follow an awkward, loose path down steep screes into Bwlch y Saethau – any attempt to drop more directly tends to be more difficult.

6 Now follow the good path across the saddle towards Y Lliwedd and then, as it bears right, **keep straight ahead** to follow the crest of the ridge which soon jacks up into a steep, scrambly path (more scrambling to the left). This leads onto Lliwedd's West Peak.

7 Continue over the East Peak and follow the escarpment along over Lliwedd Bach before the path bears left to descend steeply to join the Miner's Track by the shores of Llyn Llydaw. **Turn right** onto this and follow it easily down to the car park.

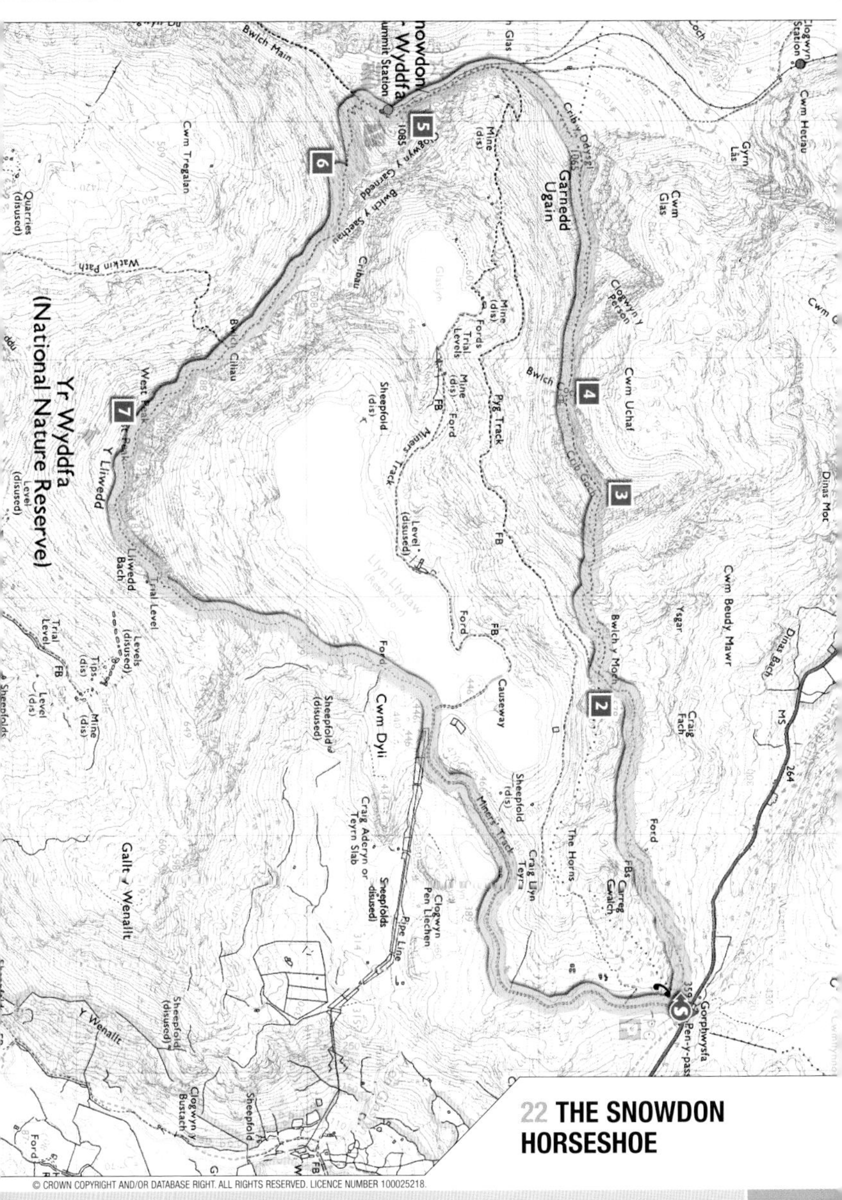

22 THE SNOWDON HORSESHOE

Also by
Vertebrate Publishing
Day Walks in the YorkshireDales
20 circular routes in the Central Pennines
Bernard Newman
Day Walks in the LakeDistrict
20 circular routes on the Lakeland Fells
Day Walks in the PeakDistrict
20 New Circular Routes
Norman Taylor & Barry Pope
Day Walks on the SouthDowns
20 circular routes in Hampshire & Sussex
Day Walks in the North York Moors
20 circular routes in North Yorkshire
Tony Harker
Order direct from www.v-publishing.co.uk

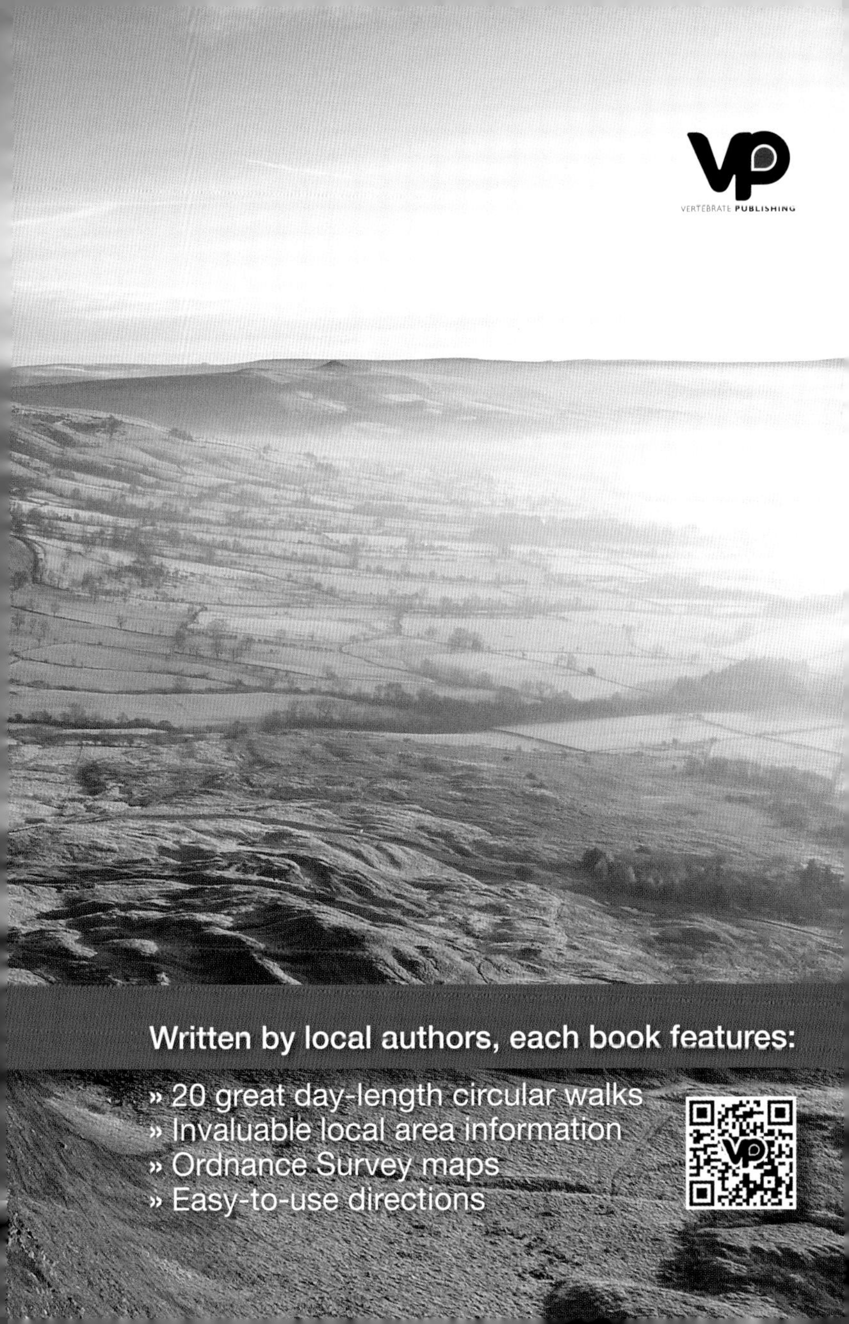

Written by local authors, each book features:

- » 20 great day-length circular walks
- » Invaluable local area information
- » Ordnance Survey maps
- » Easy-to-use directions

Appendix

The following is a list of Tourist Information Centres, shops, cafes, pubs, websites and other contacts that might come in handy.

Tourist Information Centres

www.visitsnowdonia.info – Official tourism website for the National Park.

Aberdovey (Apr–Oct)	T: 01654 767 321
Barmouth	T: 01341 280 787
Beddgelert	T: 01766 890 615
Betws-y-Coed	T: 01690 710 426
Caernarfon	T: 01286 672 232
Conwy	T: 01492 592 248
Dolgellau	T: 01341 422 888
Harlech (Apr–Oct)	T: 01766 780 658
Llandudno	T: 01492 577 577
Porthmadog	T: 01766 512 981

Food and Drink

Cafes

(There are hundreds of cafés in Snowdonia. See individual routes for recommendations.)

Pete's Eats, Llanberis	T: 01286 870 117
Y Caban, Brynrefail	T: 01286 685 500
Pinnacle Café, Capel Curig	T: 01690 720 201
Alpine Coffee Shop, Betws-y-Coed	T: 01690 710 747
Caffi Gwynant, Beddgelert	T: 01766 890 855
Caffi'r Cyfnod, Bala	T: 01678 521 260

Pubs

(See individual routes for recommendations)

The Vaynol Arms, Nant Peris	T: 01286 872 672
The Bryn Tyrch, Capel Curig	T: 01690 720 223
The Heights Hotel, Llanberis	T: 01286 871 179
Cwellyn Arms, Rhyd Ddu	T: 01766 890 321
The Cross Foxes, Brithdir	T: 01341 421 001

Accommodation

Youth Hostels

YHA Youth Hostels can be found in the following places. For more information please visit www.yha.org.uk

Betws-y-Coed	T: 01690 710 796
Bryn Gwynant	T: 0845 371 9108
Idwal Cottage	T: 0845 371 9744
Kings (Dolgellau)	T: 0845 371 9327
Llanberis	T: 0845 371 9645
Pen y Pass	T: 0845 371 9534
Rowen	T: 0845 371 9038
Snowdon Ranger	T: 0845 371 9659

Bunkhouses, B&Bs and Hotels

Some of the pubs previously listed provide accommodation. Alternatively, contact the tourist information centre closest to the area you intend to visit.

Camping

There are campsites all over Snowdonia. Here's a few to get you started:

Nant Peris Campsite	T: 01286 870 494
Bryn Tyrch Farm, Capel Curig	T: 01690 720 414
Gwern Gof Isaf, Capel Curig	T: 01690 720 276

Weather

www.metoffice.gov.uk/loutdoor/mountainsafety
www.metcheck.com

Useful Websites

www.snowdonia-active.com

Outdoor Shops

V12 Outdoor – Llanberis
T: **01286 871 534** **www.v12outdoor.com**

Joe Brown – Llanberis
T: **01286 870 327** **www.joe-brown.com**

Cunningham's – Betws-y-Coed
T: **01690 710 454** **www.srcunningham.co.uk**

Ultimate Outdoors – Betws-y-Coed
T: **01690 710 555** **www.ultimateoutdoors.co.uk**

Cotswold Outdoor – Betws-y-Coed
T: **01690 710710** **www.cotswoldoutdoor.com**

Other Publications

Day Walks in the Lake District
Stephen Goodwin, Vertebrate Publishing –
www.v-publishing.co.uk

Day Walks in the Peak District
Norman Taylor & Barry Pope,
Vertebrate Publishing – **www.v-publishing.co.uk**

Wales Mountain Biking – Beicio Mynydd Cymru
Tom Hutton, Vertebrate Publishing –
www.v-publishing.co.uk

About the Author

Tom Hutton is an award winning writer and photographer with a true passion for exploration and a love of high places. Since quitting his 'proper' job in his late 30's, his work has appeared in all the major UK outdoor publications and he has also written and illustrated a number of guidebooks. He's never happier than when he's in the mountains, whether walking, climbing, skiing or even mountain biking and he has a self-confessed unhealthy obsession with maps. He originally hails from Bristol but now lives among the mountains of Mid Wales with his journalist partner, Steph Duits and Black Labrador, Du. He is the current Chair of BMC Cymru/Wales.

Vertebrate Publishing

Vertebrate Publishing an independent publisher dedicated to producing the very best outdoor leisure titles. We have critically acclaimed and award-winning titles covering a range of leisure activities, including; mountain biking, cycling, rock climbing, hill walking and others. We are best known forour own titles such as *Lake District Mountain Biking*, and *Revelations* – the autobiography of British rock climber Jerry Moffatt, awarded the **Grand Prize** at the **2009 Banff Mountain Book Festival**.
For more information about Vertebrate Publishing please visit our website:
www.v-publishing.co.uk

CADAIR IDRIS IN WINTER

Notes